DATE DUE		

30408000005051

776
MIL

Miller, Ron.

Digital art :
painting with pixels

DIGITAL ART

PAINTING WITH PIXELS

RON MILLER

 Twenty-First Century Books • Minneapolis

This book is dedicated to my mother and father.

Acknowledgments
I am enormously grateful to master digital artists Stewart McKissick, Matt Johnson, Eric Spray, William Vaughn, Pieter Swusten, Kenji Bliss, and Scott McInnes for their help, advice, and kind permission to reproduce their work. Special thanks to Jeff Scheetz of the DAVE School and Logan DeAngelis of ComiXpress for their enthusiastic support and assistance, and to Tom Miller, without whose art and assistance this book would have been much less than it is.

Twenty-First Century Books
A division of Lerner Publishing Group, Inc.
241 First Avenue North
Minneapolis, MN 55401 U.S.A.

Website address: www.lernerbooks.com

Library of Congress Cataloging-in-Publication Data

Miller, Ron, 1947–
    Digital art : painting with pixels / by Ron Miller.
        p.   cm.
    Includes bibliographical references and index.
    ISBN 978–0–8225–7516–0 (lib. bdg. : alk. paper)
        1. Digital art—Technique—Juvenile literature. I. Title.
    N7433.8.M55 2008
    776—dc22   2007027633

Manufactured in the United States of America
1 2 3 4 5 6 – PA – 13 12 11 10 09 08

CONTENTS

A futuristic city is depicted in this digital painting by Eric Spray.

INTRODUCTION
IS IT ART?

Great debate rages about using computers to create art. People have asked questions such as "Is digital art 'real' art?" or "Is digital art 'cheating'?" These questions have led to some heated discussions.

The history of art is partly a history of technological advances. Oil paint, perspective (in which artists create a realistic sense of depth), lithography (the art of printing from a flat stone surface), the camera lucida (an instrument that allows artists to copy scenes directly from nature), photography, the airbrush, acrylics, and countless other advances all mark turning points. Some were small and affected only specialized areas of the art field. Others changed the flow of art history like a rock in a fast-flowing river. Artists adapted to some of these advances painlessly and often enthusiastically.

For instance, before the introduction of perspective, the realistic depiction of nature was not a purpose of art. Instead, artists chose the size and position of objects in a picture by their relative importance to one another. A distant castle might appear to be larger than one in the foreground because it was considered more important.

Italian artist Filippo Brunelleschi (1377–1446) created the rules of perspective in the early fifteenth century. His breakthroughs led artists to portray the world as it really looked to the human eye. Some artists, such as Albrecht Durer (1471–1528) of Germany, even went so far as to make special tools to help them create mathematically perfect perspective drawings. These were perhaps the first mechanical devices to be used to create art.

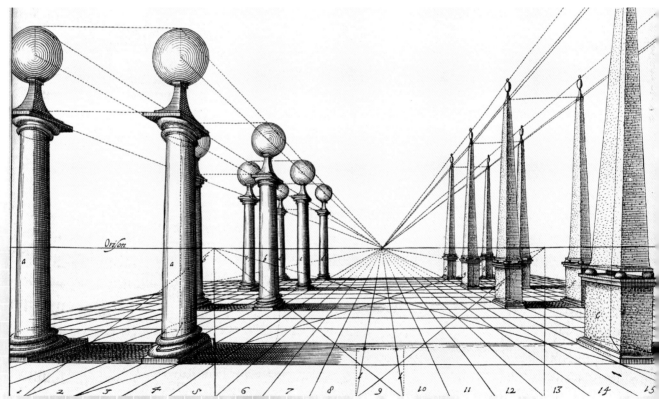

AN EARLY DEMONSTRATION OF GEOMETRIC
perspective drawn by sixteenth-century artist Jan Vredeman de Vries

DIGITAL ART

NEW MATERIALS

Before the invention of oil paints, media such as encaustics (painting with hot wax) and various forms of tempera (a water-based paint) led the field. Yet, even the oldest Mediterranean civilizations knew how to use oil to carry the colored pigments in paint. Oil had so many drawbacks, however, that some authorities discouraged its use.

Once Flemish painter Jan van Eyck perfected oils around 1410, the medium quickly became widespread. Almost all other painting materials were reduced to a secondary status. Only water-soluble acrylic paints, introduced in the 1950s, have made any dent in oil's popularity. And oil is still the preferred media of most gallery artists and many Adobe® Illustrator® users.

Occasionally, an innovation is not met with such widespread enthusiasm. After the invention of photography in the early nineteenth century, painter Paul Delaroche said that photography "completely satisfies art's every need." By this he meant that a photograph could do anything an artist could, so painters would become useless.

Delaroche reflected the feelings of many academic painters, who supported themselves by making highly lifelike paintings: portraits, landscapes, historical scenes, and so forth that pleased their rich patrons. The camera could capture scenes with an accuracy that even the finest painter could not achieve. Photography was also cheap and could be done by anyone.

Many artists, though, quickly realized the possibilities of photography, looking at it not as a rival but as an ally. For example, Eugène Delacroix (1798–1863) studied the human body by using photographs of the nude. He also worked from photographs of models when making drawings and paintings. Many other artists began doing this too since photos were much easier than living models, who not only might move while posing but also charged for their time.

Meanwhile, other artists found it advantageous to let photography take over the dull depiction of reality. It freed them to explore other realms of color, light, and composition. Impressionism and other schools of art that sprang up at the end of the nineteenth century might have been delayed by decades, if not longer, if not for the liberating influence of photography.

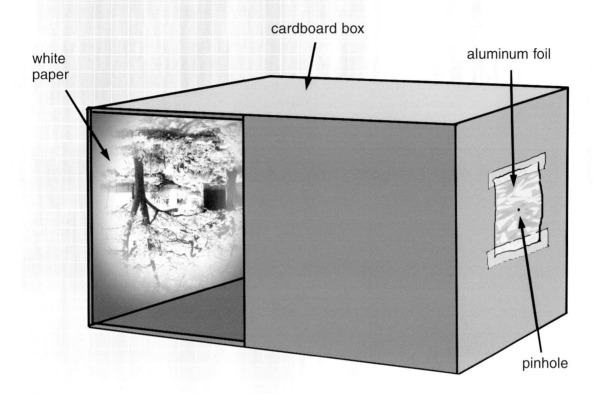

white
paper

cardboard box

aluminum foil

pinhole

A SIMPLE CAMERA OBSCURA CAN BE MADE WITH A CARDBOARD BOX,
aluminum foil, a sheet of black paper, and a sheet of white paper. Cover the inside of the box
with black paper. In the center of the box, cut a small pinhole. Cover the hole with aluminum
foil, taping or gluing it in place. Punch a small hole in the foil, and then place a sheet of white
paper inside the box opposite the hole. When light passes through the pinhole it will project
an upsidedown image of the scene in front of the camera onto the white paper inside.

MECHANICAL ASSISTANTS

Most artists quickly used new technology to create their artwork. They
have used all sorts of machines to help them create. The pantograph, for
instance, enlarges or reduces a drawing. Artists also use a camera
obscura, meaning "dark room" in Latin. These early devices were full-
size, light-tight rooms with a small hole in an outside wall. Visitors
would see an image of the surrounding landscape projected onto the
opposite wall.

Artists used this concept in a different way. They made it into a box
with a tiny pinhole in one side and a white screen opposite to it. When
the light from a scene or model passes through the pinhole, an image is

projected onto the screen. The artist can then easily trace the image. It's still a valuable tool used by modern artists.

In 1879 Abner Peeler invented the first airbrush. The airbrush uses compressed air to create a jet of very fine paint particles. By adjusting the amount of air pressure and the amount of paint, artists can create soft lines and shapes and blend colors together smoothly. The airbrush also creates incredible lighting effects. Although a very valuable tool, the airbrush has taken a great deal of abuse. Traditional painters often consider it a form of cheating.

Many professional artists dislike that nonartists can easily create beautiful effects with an airbrush. Unfortunately, the result is often beautiful effects but very bad art. Airbrush art soon became associated—unfairly—with cheap, gaudy, amateur artwork. Although it quickly became one of the most important tools of modern artists working in advertising and illustration, most other artists scorned it.

Similar attitudes of disapproval (mixed with a bit of fear) greeted the development of digital art in the 1960s. Many artists dismissed the new medium as "computer-generated art." This label suggests that computers create the art, but they do not. The computer no more creates art than a camera is responsible for the photographs it produces.

Without the photographer, the camera is just a box. It requires a human being to create a photograph. A photographer must be an artist—with an artist's sensibilities, training, skills, experience, and intelligence—to create a work of art. Without its operator, a computer is just a collection of plastic, metal, glass, and silicon. An artist needs to operate the computer to create a piece of art.

THE DIGITAL PAINTBRUSH

Like the airbrush, the computer can produce certain effects almost too easily. The nonartist can create images that are seemingly attractive but lack the artist's knowledge of color, composition, content, and more. For example, the popular software program Poser® lets both artists and nonartists create somewhat realistic human figures. The nonartist will take the figures as given, unaware of their flaws. The artist—with training and knowledge of anatomy and proportion—can see flaws and

THIS IS AN EXAMPLE of a painting that a digital artist created on the computer for a science-fiction story in a magazine.

correct them. While the flood of amateur digital art has made some people dismiss the entire genre, the reality is that it still takes an artist to make true digital art.

Some critics have also dismissed the digital genre because an "original" does not exist. The artist does not create an individual, unique object that can be hung on a wall or displayed in a gallery. This criticism would be news to great European artists such as Rembrandt, Toulouse-Lautrec, Daumier, and many others, who were certain their etchings and lithographs were genuine works of art. In fact, an entire branch of art called the graphic arts is devoted to creating art that appears in multiple copies, none of which can be pointed to as a unique "original."

But the conversation about digital art comes down to this: is it art at all? Of course, it is art. Art is what artists make. Does it matter what tools an artist uses or what materials? A painting can be created in oils, or it can be created in the artist's own blood. Gutzon Borglum sculpted Mount Rushmore from 1927 to 1941 with jackhammers and dynamite—certainly not the usual tools of an artist.

DIGITAL ART

On the other hand, using a tool or any other medium doesn't automatically mean a work of art is created—a mistake too many would-be computer artists make. One can paint a house with oil paints—that doesn't make it a work of art. A palette knife can be used to putty a window—that doesn't make the window a work of art, either. By the same token, artists can create works of art with a computer just as they can create works of art with an airbrush, a sharpened bamboo stick, their own fingers, or a jackhammer and a stick of dynamite. But an image produced by a computer isn't automatically a work of art. What makes the difference in both cases is the mind behind the keyboard and

KENJI BLISS, AN ART STUDENT AT THE COLUMBUS COLLEGE of Art and Design in Ohio, created this digital fantasy painting as part of a school assignment.

mouse. If it's an artist's mind, then what is being created is art—whether the artist is manipulating pixels or paint.

Engineers and architects got it right a long time ago when they developed programs to help them create technical drawings. No one has ever suggested that a computer itself designed a skyscraper or airplane. No one has suggested that a building or airplane is any less viable because its architect or engineer used a computer program to create the design. A computer left all alone in a room isn't going to do anything but hum along until it goes into standby mode. It's not going to suddenly blink with inspiration and start writing books and creating artwork. It needs an artist to do that. So perhaps we need to do nothing more than simply stop using the phrase "computer-*generated* art" and start calling it by its right name: computer-*aided* art.

This is a fractal image that Ron Miller created on his computer.

CHAPTER ONE

THE ARCHAEOLOGY OF DIGITAL ART

So what is digital art? Let's define digital art as anything of a visual nature that artists created with the aid of a computer. By "digital" we mean the computer uses numbers (digits) to translate and record information. For example, when you take a photograph with a digital camera, you are creating a digital code. The camera captures the shot and translates it into a numeric code. To the human eye, the photo could be an image of a person or a tree. To a computer, the photo is a code containing billions of numbers. Once this code is recorded, or saved, the numbers can be used to make exact duplicates of the original artwork. Or the code can be changed to create changes in the art.

Scientists have been using the connection between the visual and the numerical for quite some time. For more than a century, scientists have used machines to translate numerical data into visual form. The oscilloscope—which detects electrical pulses and translates them into waves on a screen—is probably the very earliest such machine. German scientist Karl Ferdinand Braun developed the first oscilloscope in 1897. The basic technology of Braun's invention included the cathode-ray tube—which eventually became the television tube.

Naturally, some creative minds saw art in the oscilloscope's perfectly shaped waves. An oscilloscope artist created special wave shapes by changing the data input to the device. Gifted artists could produce spectacular waves of complex lines. But the only way to save an oscilloscope image was to take a photograph of the oscilloscope screen.

THE BEGINNING

American scientists built the first big computers in the 1940s and 1950s. But these were strictly calculating machines. In fact, they were unbelievably huge and expensive calculating machines. For example, a 1950s-era computer filled an entire room—if not an entire building—and cost millions of dollars. (And those old machines had less computing power than a modern five-dollar handheld calculator available at your local discount store!) They created curves and graphs for mathematicians and engineers.

The early computers of the late 1940s and 1950s output data through typewriter-like devices. They usually output columns of numbers and letters. These letters and numbers could be seen as areas of light and dark. For instance, an *m* or *x* looks darker on the page than an *o*, *i*, or dot. Pictures could be created if users fed the right numbers into the computer.

By using combinations of many different characters, users could create complex and surprisingly realistic images. The process was very similar to the way black-and-white photos are reproduced in newspapers, magazines, and books. The photo is broken up into tiny dots. The size of the dot determines how dark it is. Small dots have a lot of white around them and look lighter, while larger dots make a space look darker.

CREATING DIGITAL ART WITHOUT COMPUTERS

Two devices create patterns like oscilloscopes through purely mechanical means. The harmonograph was a very popular household item in the late nineteenth century. The Spirograph is a popular toy that has been sold in stores for more than forty years.

The harmonograph uses the principle of the pendulum to make complex patterns of swirling lines. The simplest harmonograph uses a pendulum swinging over an area of smooth sand. As the pendulum swings, a point on the end traces out patterns in the sand. Mathematicians call these patterns Lissajous figures.

In other versions, the pendulum's bob consists of a large cone (such as a paper cup) filled with

ONE OF THE SIMPLEST FORMS

of a harmonograph is shown at *right*. When set swinging, the sand dribbling from the cone creates a figure-8 pattern *(below)*.

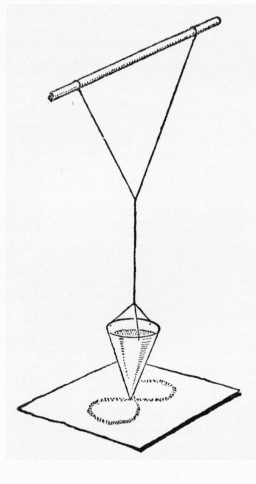

THIS IS AN EXAMPLE
of the complex and beautiful patterns that artists can create with a harmonograph. This particular image was created using a computer version of the instrument.

fine sand. The sand drains from a small hole in its point. Very complex patterns result when several pendulum actions are combined, such as when one pendulum swings from another. A harmonograph that creates really complex patterns can be quite large—though still simple to build.

In 1966 the Kenner toy company introduced the Spirograph in the United States. The simple toy has several geared plastic wheels and toothed rings that can create beautiful curves. The toy is based on a type of mathematical curve called a trochoid. A trochoid is the path of a point fixed relative to a circle that is rolling along a straight line.

Imagine a reflector attached to one of the spokes of a bicycle wheel. When the wheel turns, the reflector makes a circle as it rotates around the hub. But if the bicycle is moving relative to the ground, the reflector follows a curve that looks like a series of arcs. Imagine the cyclist was part of a circus act and drove her bike around the inside of a large curved track. Then the reflector would trace out an even more complex curve called an epicycloid. If more circles are added, the curves become even more complex.

A plotter is another device that creates images with the computer. It is a pen that the computer moves over a sheet of paper in two directions: up and down and back and forth. By combining these two motions, users can make the computer draw complex curves. Plotters can produce very detailed work, as well as work of very large dimensions. People soon realized that computers could be used to make curves and graphs that were visually appealing. Thus, the computer might be a tool for creating art.

THE FIRST ATTEMPTS

The first tools used to make electronic art—a predecessor to digital art—were originally designed for testing sound equipment. The company that became the Hewlett Packard Company developed the first of these products, an audio oscillator. This instrument creates one pure tone, or frequency, at a time. The waves that this tone produces can be displayed on the screen of an oscilloscope. The patterns on the oscilloscope screen give scientists and engineers information about the wave and its source.

Ben Laposky, an artist and mathematician from Cherokee, Iowa, realized that by changing the input he could create patterns of his own design. In 1950 he created the first graphic images made by an electronic machine. Laposky captured his electronic oscilloscope imagery by photographing it onto high-speed film. He called them oscillons and electronic abstractions.

Meanwhile, the Viennese artist Herbert W. Franke also created electronic images. Franke's images were similar to those of Laposky's but reflected his own artistic sensibilities and goals. Franke eventually wrote the first book on digital art: *Computer Graphics-Computer Art* (1971).

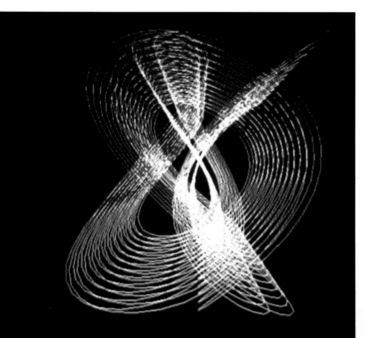

THIS COMPUTER-GENERATED harmonograph image is similar to the designs produced by an oscilloscope and the oscillons created by Ben Laposky.

CHLADNI FIGURES

In 1787 the German physicist Ernst Chladni found that when he drew a violin bow against the edge of a metal plate covered with fine sand *(right)*, complex patterns would form in the sand. Depending on where the plate was stroked by the bow, he could create different patterns. The practical application of Chladni's discovery has been in the design of musical instruments. But the patterns in themselves *(below)* are pleasing and are perhaps one of the earliest examples of machine-generated art.

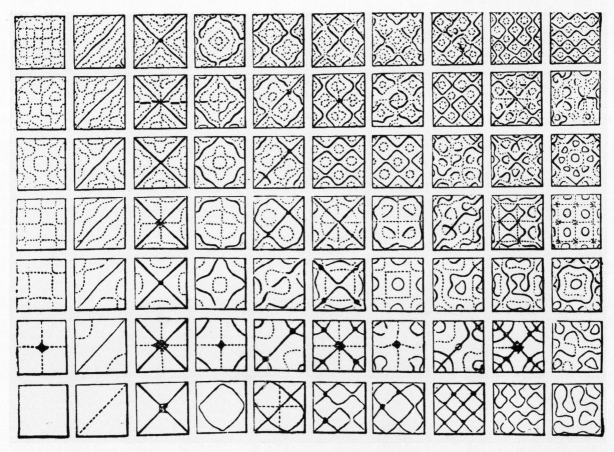

THE GOLDEN RATIO

A link between math and art has been clear since the early Greeks used mathematical ratios to construct temples and buildings. One such ratio—called the divine proportion, or the golden ratio—created such pleasing proportions that it is still used. A ratio of length to width of approximately 1.618 (a rectangle with sides of 1 unit and 1.618 units) has long been considered the most visually appealing.

The golden ratio can be found everywhere. The ancient Greeks, who not only discovered the golden ratio but were fascinated by it, used it in their architecture. For example, the ratio can be found throughout the famous Parthenon in Athens. Also, the standard credit card is 2.12 by

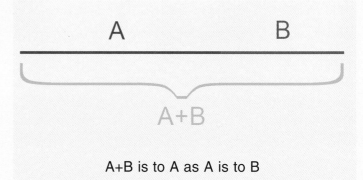

A+B is to A as A is to B

THE GOLDEN RATIO IS BASED

on the line above. The ratio of A plus B together compared to A is the same as the ratio of A and B. The Parthenon (below) was built in Athens, Greece, in the fifth century B.C. Its proportions were based on the golden rectangle, which in turn is based on the golden ratio.

3.38 inches (54 by 86 millimeters)—a ratio of 0.628, less than a millimeter off from a perfect golden ratio.

This ratio appears not only in art and architecture but in nature as well. The proportions of the golden ratio can be found in the spiraling shape of the seeds in the center of a sunflower, the leaves and spikes of a pineapple, and the arrangement of the seed cases on a pinecone. Many of the proportions of the human body fit the golden ratio—the length of the hand, for instance, compared to the length of the forearm or the distance from the feet to the top of the head compared to the distance from the feet to the navel.

MODERN ARCHITECTURE,

such as the United Nations Building in New York, is often based on the golden rectangle. Even the individual windows in the tower are golden rectangles.

John Whitney Sr., who studied music and photography, closely followed Laposky's and Franke's work. In the 1940s, Whitney created an experimental film with his brother James that won first prize at a film festival in Belgium. His work in 1955 as a director of animation at the famous UPA cartoon studios led him to a partnership with Saul Bass. (Bass is probably best known for the opening title sequences he designed for the early James Bond films.) Together they created the title sequence for the Alfred Hitchcock film *Vertigo* (1958), as well as graphics for television shows.

In 1960 Whitney founded Motion Graphics Incorporated. The company used a computer to produce motion picture and television sequences and commercials. Whitney had built the computer himself from war-surplus electronics. Gradually it evolved into a huge machine that towered 12 feet (3.6 meters) high. Whitney continued to perfect his computer and the effects it created.

In 1961 Whitney produced a seven-minute color film called *Catalog*. In this film, he showed all the effects he had perfected with his homemade computer. Whitney achieved worldwide recognition for his work with the analog computer. In 1966 IBM awarded him the company's first artist-in-residence status, allowing him to freely explore the potential of computer graphics.

ARTISTS DISCOVER THE COMPUTER

By the mid-1960s, some artists began to explore ways to combine computer technology with art. Until then artistical experiments with computers had been more or less limited to engineers. Only they had the technical expertise to use computers. The interactive software that is so readily available in modern times didn't exist. Programs had to be created from scratch, custom built for each individual computer.

Also, computers were not readily available. Until the 1970s, computers were enormous and very expensive. For instance, Sketchpad was the first program specifically designed to create drawings. Ivan Sutherland developed the program at the Massachusetts Institute of Technology (MIT) in 1963 on one of the most advanced computers of the time. The machine itself occupied 1,000 square feet (93 sq. m) of space. It had a main memory of 320 kilobytes—that is, 320,000 units of information—stored in a memory core about 1 cubic yard (0.8 cu. m) in size. Users fed the computer programs on a punched paper tape while the drawings appeared on a 7-inch (18-centimeter) black-and-white monitor. By comparison, a modern desktop computer that costs only a few hundred dollars may have up to 200 gigabytes of memory. That's 200 billion units, more than a quarter million times that of the computer used by Sketchpad!

In spite of this, many artists and scientists became successful partners in the creation of the first computer-aided artwork. But this collaboration was long in coming. Scientists held the first exhibitions of computer art in 1965 and featured only work created by scientists. Two years later, however, artists Billy Kluver and Robert Rauschenberg founded an organization called Experiments in Art and Technology (EAT). The organization, funded in part by Bell Laboratories (later Luminent), tried to bridge the gap between artists and scientists. A number of important avant-garde artists, including Robert Rauschenberg, Andy Warhol, Jasper Johns, and composer John Cage, contributed work.

The work of these very famous artists could be found in major museums and galleries all around the world. Not surprisingly, these particular artists embraced the new technology. Most of them had already been using new technologies in creating their art, so the move to digital art was probably both easy and natural. Rauschenberg, for instance, created elaborate montages with the help of photographic techniques. Warhol employed the halftone processes used in creating photos in newspapers and magazines. And John Cage had long been interested in electronic music. The interest in digital art from these respected artists gave the form a kind of official seal of approval. People who once scorned the use of computers in creating art became interested in it.

In 1968 Jasia Reichardt created a two-month-long exhibition called Cybernetic Serendipity at the Institute of Contemporary Arts in London, England. It included work by 325 artists and scientists from around the world, including important work by John Cage, John Whitney Sr., Charles Csuri, Michael Noll, and many others. After closing in London, the exhibition went to Washington, D.C., and San Francisco, California. While not the first such exhibition, it was one of the largest. It made the art world and the general public fully aware of computer and electronic art.

THE EARLY DIGITAL ARTISTS

In 1968 Hungarian artist Vera Molnar began using the computer to transform basic geometric shapes, such as squares, circles, and triangles. She rotated them, deformed them, erased parts, or combined different shapes into new ones. Then she printed her final results with a plotter. "Proceeding by small steps," she said, "the painter is in a position to delicately pinpoint the image of dreams. Without the aid of a computer, it would not be possible to materialize quite so faithfully an image that previously existed only in the artist's mind. This may sound paradoxical, but the machine, which is thought to be cold and inhuman, can help to realize what is most subjective, unattainable, and profound in a human being."

In 1969 German artist Manfred Mohr turned from traditional painting to the computer. He worked on variations of the cube, which he distorted and transformed endlessly. Mohr worked only in black and white, using a plotter to print his work. In 1971 the Musée d'Art Moderne de la Ville de Paris gave him a one-man show. It was the first such honor from any museum for a computer artist.

Larry Cuba is a widely known pioneer of computer animation. He created his first film, *First Fig*, in 1974. Computers capable of digital art were not easy to come by at that time. So Cuba joined with computer scientists at the National Aeronautics and Space Administration's Jet Propulsion Laboratory in Pasadena, California. In 1975 John Whitney Sr. invited Cuba to work with him on the movie *Arabesque*. Later films, such as *3/78 (Objects and Transformations)* (1978), *Two Space* (1979), and *Calculated Movements* (1985) have been shown all over the world.

Lillian Schwartz pioneered the use of computers in graphics, film, video, animation, special effects, virtual reality, and multimedia. Her work was the first in the new medium of computer-aided art to be bought by the Museum of Modern Art in New York. The museum used her sculpture, *Proxima Centauri*, in its 1968 Machine Exhibition.

Independently and in collaboration with scientists at Bell Labs, Schwartz later developed ways to use computers in film and animation. Her award-winning films—such as *Mirage* (1974)—have been shown all over the world. Schwartz has also constructed three-dimensional models. One such model will help art historians study the perspective used by

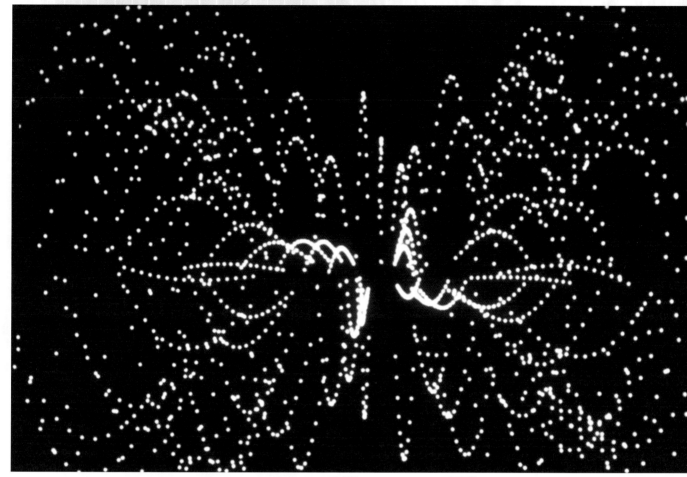

AN IMAGE FROM LARRY CUBA'S FILM
3/78 (Objects and Transformations), **released in 1978**

Leonardo da Vinci in creating his famous fifteenth-century painting *Last Supper*. More recently, she created a digital model of the Leaning Tower of Pisa that will help preserve the famous structure.

Yoichiro Kawaguchi, one of the leading international computer artists, originally teamed up with computer scientists. With their help, he developed art using metaballs. This technology, invented by Jim Blinn, created soft, fluid, organic shapes. Before this, most computer artists were limited to hard-edged geometric shapes. The patterns Kawaguchi found in natural forms, such as seashells and plants, inspired him. He won many international honors and awards for his art and animation.

Ed Emshwiller is a famous science-fiction illustrator. He was also a highly respected video artist and dean of the School of Film/Video at the California Institute of the Arts in Valencia. He helped influence the experimental film movement in the 1960s. Many of his films, including *Thanatopsis* (1962), *Totem* (1963), *Relativity* (1966), and *Three Dancers* (1970), received awards and screenings at film festivals in cities around the world.

In 1987 Emshwiller created *Hungers*, an electronic video opera, for the Los Angeles Arts Festival. *Hungers* combined live performance and interactive devices that changed the sound of the music according to the environment. No two performances were exactly alike.

FRACTALS

Another major advance in digital art occurred when mathematicians discovered fractals. While fractals involve complex math, the basic concept is simple. But before trying to define fractals, let's present an example that you can do with a pencil and paper.

Start with an equilateral triangle. Divide one side of the triangle into three equal parts, and remove the middle section. Replace it with two lines the same length as the section you just removed. Do this to all three sides of the triangle. The result will be a six-pointed star. Do this again with the twelve new sides you've created. And do it again and again. . . . The resulting figure is called a Koch snowflake, after the Swedish mathematician Helge von Koch, who first described it in 1904.

Fractals are special because they look the same at any scale. A close-up of any detail of a fractal looks just like a larger section. You can zoom in as much as you like, and the fractal will always look the same. Fractals can be found throughout nature. A branch of a tree, for instance, looks like the entire tree. A rock looks like the mountain it was found on. The indentations of a coastline seen from space look like the indentations of a coastline seen from only a few feet away or even when seen under a magnifying glass.

For more than half a century, mathematicians working on complex fractals rarely knew what they might actually look like. Mathematicians were only able to make rough sketches by hand, so it wasn't possible to make out their true intricacy. When mathematicians first plotted fractals with computers in the late 1960s, they finally discovered their amazing beauty—and artists quickly realized their potential.

NATURAL FRACTALS

The relationship of fractals in math to fractals in the natural world is one of the reasons artists have been so successful in re-creating natural scenes digitally. Fractals can be found throughout nature, from the snowflake to the shoreline. Perhaps the perfect example of this is the vegetable romanesco broccoli. It is formed of many small, bumpy knobs. Each of these knobs looks like the entire head and is in turn formed of even smaller knobs. These smaller knobs are themselves tiny versions of the larger ones . . . and on and on almost as small as the eye can see. The arrangement of all the parts of the broccoli closely resembles a fractal called the Sierpinski triangle.

THIS BROCCOLI IS AN IDEAL example of fractal forms in nature. No matter how closely you look at the vegetable, the details resemble the entire thing.

THIS "SNOWFLAKE"

illustrates how fractals are built from simple geometric forms. Each side of the triangle at the top left has a triangle added to it to make the second form. Then each of those sides has a smaller triangle added to it. This can be done indefinitely, making the figure quite complex. However, no matter how infinitely small the details get, each small part resembles the larger, original shape.

Elaborate snowflakes might hardly seem to be the basis for any kind of art form. But other mathematicians who were working on fractals, such as Benoit B. Mandelbrot and Gaston Julia, produced astonishing results. Until then, most fractals were very symmetrical and artificial looking. Many of the more complex fractal types look very different as you zoom in. They still reflect qualities of the original form, but not so strictly. This means that as you zoom into the figure, the shapes will always be changing while staying similar to the full-size image. This is much more like fractals in the natural world. A tree branch may resemble the tree it came from, but it won't be an exact copy.

A SMALL PART OF A FRACTAL DESIGN RESEMBLES THE ENTIRE THING.

When the small area outlined in the image *(below left)* is enlarged *(below middle)*, it looks like the original. When a small area of that selection is enlarged *(below right)*, it still looks nearly the same.

DIGITAL NATURE

Digital artists use fractals to create special visual effects that are then used in their artwork. Often fractals are used for their natural beauty. But one of the most important uses of fractals goes directly to the fractal core of natural forms. Software designers realized that the math of fractals can be used to describe natural forms such as clouds, trees, rocks, and shorelines. So they developed programs that create extraordinarily realistic digital landscapes. Images created by programs such as Terragen™, for example, are sometimes impossible to tell apart from photographs of real landscapes.

A DIGITAL ARTIST CREATED THIS REALISTIC
landscape of an alien planet using fractal-based software.

DIGITAL ART

A COMPUTER-GENERATED FRACTAL image *(left)* closely resembles the shape and form of a natural branch of leaves *(below)*. Many forms in nature are fractal. Here, one of the large branches of leaves resembles an individual smaller cluster. The fact that natural objects have so many fractal features enables digital artists to use computer-generated fractals to emulate natural forms.

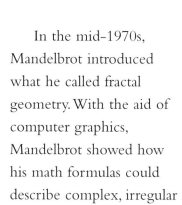

In the mid–1970s, Mandelbrot introduced what he called fractal geometry. With the aid of computer graphics, Mandelbrot showed how his math formulas could describe complex, irregular natural forms. Examples of these are the formation of clouds, the distribution of leaves and twigs on a tree, the shape of a coastline, or the spiraling form of a seashell. To do this, he had to develop not only new math concepts but also had to develop some of the first computer programs capable of printing graphics.

By this time, many artists realized the potential of the computer as a tool. But the widespread use and development of digital art had to wait until technicians created software that would work on any computer. Also, small, less expensive computers had to become widely available. This did not occur on a wide scale until the 1980s.

FRACTALS

Fractals are generated by math equations that work something like this: Every point on the monitor screen is given a unique number. These numbers are plugged into the equation, which changes them. That result is then plugged right back into the same equation. The process is like making a photocopy of a photocopy of a photocopy. Every time the image is repeated, it looks a little different. If you do this enough times, the final result will be unrecognizable from the original. By coloring the points on the screen according to preset rules, complex patterns and shapes will evolve.

To generate a single fractal image, an individual point may be run through the process a thousand times or more. Since even a small image may have more than three hundred thousand points, that's a total of three hundred million calculations. A large image may require trillions of calculations. You can understand why no one appreciated the full beauty of fractals until computers were invented. It would take many mathematicians many years to perform similar calculations.

These equations can involve extremely complex mathematics. But artists don't need to know anything about them to use fractals. In the same way, it is not necessary to understand how a television or telephone works to use it.

BY INTRODUCING some randomness into their fractals, computer artists can create designs *(left)* that increasingly resemble natural forms, such as the branching of this twig *(below)*.

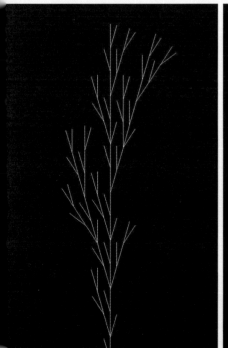

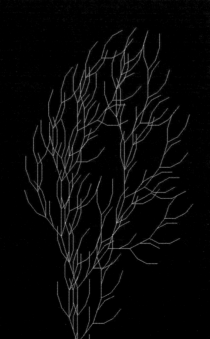

This is a CAD image of a spacecraft created by digital artist Tom Miller.

CHAPTER TWO

CAD: COMPUTER-AIDED DRAWING

The first widespread commercial application of digital art was the introduction of CAD—computer-aided design (or computer-aided drawing or computer-aided drafting, depending on what the user was doing). CAD assists engineers and designers in a wide variety of industries. It helps in designing and manufacturing products ranging from buildings, bridges, roads, aircraft, ships, and cars to digital cameras, mobile phones, computers, and clothing.

Before the advent of computer-aided drawing, designers, drafters, and

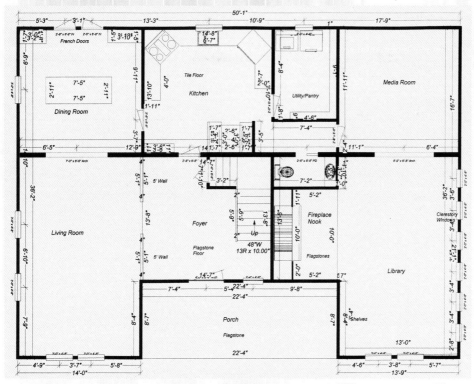

ARCHITECTS CAN USE COMPUTER-AIDED

drafting software to create building plans far more quickly, accurately, and cheaply than drawing them by hand.

engineers did all of their work entirely by hand. All the drawings on which every new invention—every airplane, every car, every building, and every piece of machinery—was based had to be done in pencil, pen, and ink. This required not only very skilled people but people skilled in the use of a great many specialized tools.

The invention of every new product involved a lengthy and difficult process. In many instances, such as of a large building or a complex machine, dozens of drafters created hundreds of drawings. If they made an error or needed to make a change, ink lines had to be erased and redrawn. Sometimes entire drawings had to be redone from scratch. Engineers and drafters welcomed the development of CAD technology, which eliminated these problems. The result was not only better, more accurate art but greater productivity. Drafters needed only a fraction of the time to create a drawing as was required before the advent of CAD.

DIGITAL ART IS WIDELY USED BY ENGINEERS

and designers to create new products and to illustrate how they work.
Phantom views such as this one by Stewart McKissick show how realistic
the results can be.

A NEW TOOL

Ivan Sutherland's program Sketchpad proved that computers could automate repetitive design and drafting tasks. The program had a reliability and accuracy that was not possible using manual methods. Drafters no longer had to draw objects over and over again by hand. Instead, they needed only copy their first drawing and paste it back in as many times as necessary. For instance, a drafter didn't have to draw every tooth in a gear—just one and then repeat it. One of Sutherland's most important achievements with Sketchpad was the light pen. A small pen with a light on its tip let users interact with the computer. They could draw directly on the monitor as though they were drawing with a pencil on a piece of paper.

Sketchpad also proved that computers could be used not just for engineering and drafting. They could be used interactively by designers—and potentially artists—in product development and design. However, computers were still large and expensive. Only big corporations—such as car manufacturers or the aerospace industry—could afford to use CAD. For instance, the first commercially available CAD program, Digigraphics, could be run only on a computer produced by the software's creator. It cost half a million dollars.

But by the end of the 1960s and the beginning of the 1970s, many software suppliers began offering CAD programs. The wider availability and competition drove down prices. Companies also developed programs with growing capabilities. Meanwhile, the first three-dimensional modeling programs also became available. Programmers designed them strictly for engineers. They were finally able to examine, for example, a machine part from all sides and angles before approving a drawing.

CAD PROGRAMS

By the end of the 1970s, computer companies introduced the first low-cost minicomputers—what became known as a personal computer (PC), or a desktop computer. IBM shipped its first PC in 1981. Companies no longer needed large, expensive, custom-built machines. Software companies were free to develop programs that could be used by a wide variety of people.

BEZIER CURVES

The tool that makes computer-aided drawing possible is the Bezier curve (named for Pierre Bezier, who developed it in the 1970s for CAD operations). This tool lets designers create extremely accurate drawings using complex curves with great precision.

The designer creates control points along the line that is being drawn. These control points allow the designer to control the shape, direction, and amount of curve. And since Bezier curves are vector graphics, they can be enlarged to any size without loss of detail or smoothness, allowing designers to fine-tune their creations. Bezier curves are not only the basis for engineering and architectural drawing programs but for art software such as Adobe Illustrator and CorelDRAW® as well.

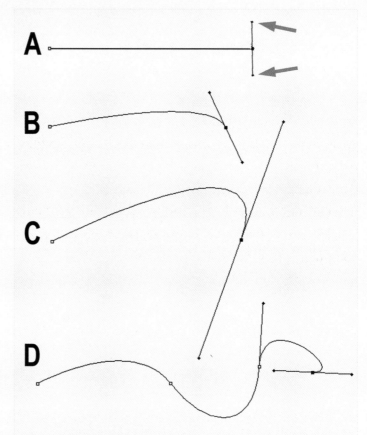

BEZIER CURVES ALLOW DESIGNERS

to create precise, accurate curves. Every Bezier line has control handles (arrows) at the end of a crosspiece (A). Moving these points will curve the line to any degree and any direction (B, C). By using as many control points as needed, the designer can create complex curves (D).

This made their software much less expensive. Autodesk® demonstrated the first CAD software for the PC, AutoCAD® 1.0, in November 1982.

Since then, many CAD programs have been published. Some are meant for highly technical professional use, while others are user friendly for the average person. An aerospace engineer might use one of the high-end products to design the turbojet engine of a new airplane. A homeowner might use an off-the-shelf program to help design a new kitchen.

Once CAD programs became readily affordable, many companies reduced the number of drafters they employed. One CAD operator could easily replace at least four or five drafters using traditional methods. Additionally, many engineers began to do their own drafting, further eliminating traditional drafting departments.

The adoption of CAD studios, or paperless studios, in architectural schools met resistance, however. Teachers worried that sketching on a computer screen did not strengthen the skills associated with the age-old practice of sketching on paper. Also, many teachers worried that students would be hired for their computer skills rather than their design skills, a worry that turned out to be justified in the early years of CAD. This problem exists not only within architecture and engineering but in many other fields of digital art. Someone will be hired less for their creative ability than for their skill with the computer. Unfortunately, this all too often shows in the finished work, which might be carefully prepared but otherwise mediocre.

Education in CAD has become accepted in almost all architecture schools. However, not all architects have wanted to join the CAD revolution. Many architects still prefer to do their designs on paper with traditional tools.

HOW IT WORKS

CAD and other drawing software depend on a system called vector graphics. This simply means that a drawing is defined by its geometry. Images created this way use geometrical primitives—or basic shapes—such as points, lines, curves, and polygons.

VIRTUAL MODELS

Engineers, architects, and designers can create three-dimensional models with CAD programs. These models can be tested almost like the real thing. Not having to actually build a machine or building to test it saves a great deal of time, effort, and money. Although computer models are no substitute for testing the real thing, they help designers get very precise information under controlled conditions.

Designers can test an aircraft, automobile, machine, building, or bridge in ways that might be difficult, dangerous, or even impossible in real life. For instance, no architect wants to wait for a real earthquake to see how a building will react. A bridge designer can determine how a design will hold up under any wind speed, not just what nature might provide. Virtual models, such as these, let engineers and architects design much more efficient, safe, and economical products than ever before.

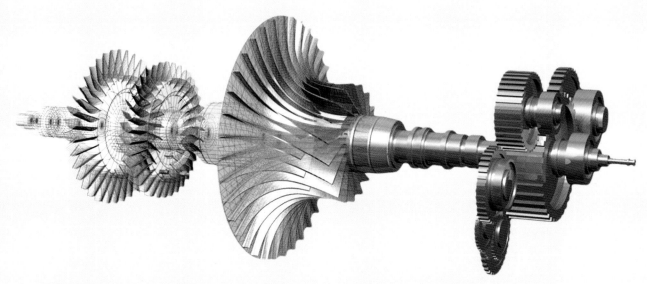

ENGINEERS WERE AMONG THE FIRST PROFESSIONAL TO USE

digital art. Instead of spending days or even weeks laboriously drawing plans for complex new machines, for instance, the same thing could instead be done in hours with **CAD**. Better yet, the finished digital drawing could be viewed from any angle as a three-dimensional object *(above)*. **(Art courtesy of Tom Miller)**

All of these are based on math equations. For instance, to create a circle, the computer needs to know:

- the radius *(r)* of the circle,
- the location of the center point of the circle,
- the style of the line and its color,
- and the color and style of any shade that might fill the circle.

No matter how much the circle is enlarged or reduced, it will always appear as sharp as it was originally. The computer is not enlarging a picture of the circle but rather the mathematics of the circle itself. The computer treats every shape and line the same way: as a geometric definition. This quality of vector graphics is of great advantage to drafters who consider accuracy crucial.

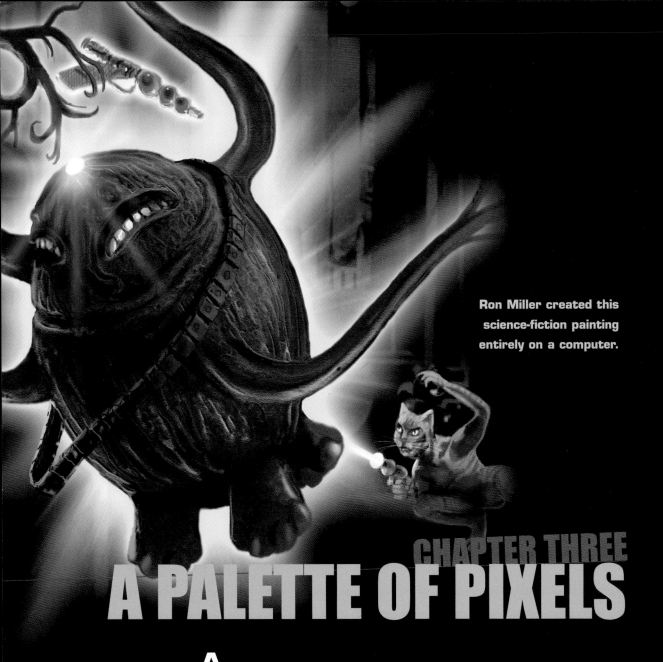

Ron Miller created this
science-fiction painting
entirely on a computer.

CHAPTER THREE

A PALETTE OF PIXELS

An image on a computer screen is made up of tiny picture elements—called pixels for short. The ordinary screen might contain over 1.3 million pixels. They cover it like a checkerboard made up of countless little squares that are almost too small to be seen with the naked eye.

The basic idea of the pixel is not too different from that of the halftone photos in the newspaper. What appear to be continuous tones of gray are—if you look closely—really just collections of small dots, each a different shade. Likewise, every pixel in a computer image is a

THE TRADITIONAL HALFTONE

process used in newspapers, books, and magazines reproduces pictures by converting them into patterns of tiny dots *(top)*. Computers can reproduce photos in a way similar to the halftone process. But instead of breaking the image up into small, different-sized black dots, the computer breaks the image up into small squares, each of which is a different shade of gray *(bottom)*. These small squares are pixels. Each square is assigned a number that tells the computer what shade of gray to use.

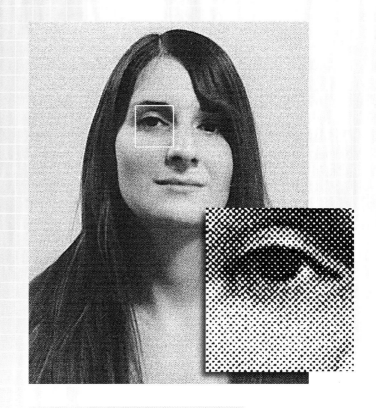

different shade of gray or a different color. Seen from a distance, they all merge together (like the newspaper photo) into continuous tones.

Each pixel is given an individual number that indicates its position on the screen—like the coordinates of a city on a map—and its color. As you might expect, even a small picture adds up to a huge list of numbers. This is why a large color picture—containing a vast amount of information—can take up so much space on a hard drive. Black-and-white pictures require less information because all that needs to be recorded is the position of a pixel and its shade of gray.

On the other hand, a color pixel needs three numbers to define its color: one each to indicate how much red, green, and blue. For instance, a

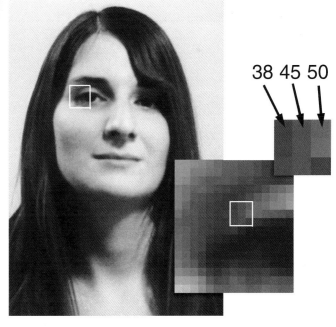

38 45 50

Red: 63
Green: 31
Blue: 27

PIXELS ARE ALSO USED
to create color images. Where only one
number was required for each pixel in a
black-and-white picture, three numbers
are needed per pixel in color images. This
three-fold increase in information is one
of the reasons that color images require
more computer file space than black-and-
white images.

bright red might be indicated by the number "250,2,2." This means that it
is made up of 250 parts of red, 2 of green, and 2 of blue. This system is
called RGB for "red, green, blue."

HOW IT WORKS

Paint programs use a system called raster graphics. Unlike vector graphics,
raster imaging is based on pixels. Raster images are stored in a computer as
a grid made up of pixels. The pixels contain the image's color and
brightness information as a series of numbers.

A raster graphics image is a rectangular grid of pixels. The color of
each pixel is individually defined. For instance, colored pixels may be
defined by three bytes—one byte each for red, green, and blue. An image
with only black-and-white pixels needs only a single bit for each pixel. (A
bit—from "**b**inary dig**it**"—is the basic unit of computer information. A bit
is either a 1 or a 0. A byte is 8 bits.)

Software programs called image editors can change the pixels to
enhance the image in many ways. The program alters the pixels by
changing the numbers that describe them. Computer users can change the
pixels individually or as a group.

DITHERING

In the past, artists displayed and printed digital images using a technique called dithering. Early monitors and printers could not handle a wide range of colors or tones of gray. To make it easier to display and print colors, they would reduce tones to just a few shades of gray or a few hundred colors (as opposed to the millions of colors that modern monitors and printers use). This did not create very attractive pictures. The transition from one color to another or one shade of gray to another would usually make a hard line. To achieve a softer and more realistic transition, tones would be dithered, or broken down into a pattern of tiny dots. Colors and grays blended into one another, giving the illusion of more colors in the picture than there really were.

Dithering worked well with early printers, which were limited in the number of colors they could print. Many of these were dot matrix printers that used a group of tiny pins arranged in a square or rectangle (3 by 3 in the first dot matrix printers to 4 by 6 in later models) to transfer ink to paper. The tiny dots these made were perfect for dithered images, which were also groups of tiny dots arranged in rectangles. This was not ideal, though, since dithered images have a speckled appearance and don't reproduce detail very well. Still, dithering gave early computer artists the chance to work with more than just solid lines and areas of color.

EXAMPLES OF DITHERING

show how small geometric grids of black-and-white squares can be used to create large areas of different gray tones (*above*). If colors are substituted for black and white, tones of color can be created. Examples of black-and-white and color dithering are shown below. Because the dots are necessarily fairly large, dithering doesn't show detail very well.

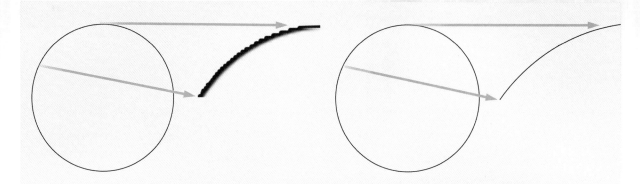

ALTHOUGH A VECTOR IMAGE ALLOWS FOR BETTER COLORS AND shading, it cannot be enlarged without edges becoming "jaggy" *(left)*. While a raster image doesn't handle shading as well, it can be enlarged as much as desired without losing resolution *(right)*. Vector images are preferred for photos and digital paintings, while raster images are preferred for technical drawings.

The total number of pixels (resolution) and the amount of information in each pixel (often called color depth) determines the quality of a raster image. For example, an image that stores the standard 24 bits of color information per pixel can represent smoother degrees of shading than one that stores only 16 bits per pixel. But it wouldn't be as smooth as one that stores 48 bits. Likewise, an image 640 by 480 pixels in size (307,200 pixels) will look rough and jaggy compared to one that is 1,280 by 1,024 in size (1,310,720 pixels).

The more information a raster image contains, however, the larger the file is. This is one of the disadvantages of the raster system. It requires much more storage space than an image created by vector graphics. Also, unlike vector graphics, raster graphics cannot be scaled to a higher resolution without losing some quality. However, raster graphics are much better at showing photos and artwork than vector graphics.

Software called raster graphics editors, which came much later than CAD software, let artists and designers paint and edit pictures with their computers. Koala Technologies released one of the earliest programs called KoalaPainter in 1983. The company originally meant for it to be used by schools, but it became very popular with home users. It came with the KoalaPad, an early graphics tablet. Instead of a pen, however, artists used their fingertips. KoalaPainter (called PC Design when used with IBM PC computers) offered thirty-two colors along with eight tools.

In 1985 the ZSoft Corporation introduced PC Paintbrush (also known as Paintbrush). Like KoalaPainter, it worked in only a limited number of colors (although the third version offered 256 colors). It was, however, one of the first examples of PC software to use a mouse.

While paint programs have grown incredibly complex since KoalaPainter and PC Paintbrush, they all have many of the same basic functions. They allow artists to:

- Select a region for editing.
- Draw lines with brushes of different color, size, shape, and pressure.
- Fill in a region with a single color, gradient of colors, or a texture.
- Select a color using different color models or by using a color "eyedropper."
- Add typed letters in different font styles.
- Remove scratches, dirt, wrinkles, and imperfections from photo images.

RASTER GRAPHICS

To show how your computer creates an image from pixels, here is the letter *R* as it might appear on your computer monitor:

R

If you look very closely at the letter, it will look something like this:

A computer, however, sees the letter like this, where 0 represents a white block and a 1 represents a black block:

111110
100001
100001
100001
111110
100100
100010
100001

Wherever an 0 appears, the computer inserts the current background color. Where a 1 appears, it inserts the current foreground color. You will notice that each block—or pixel—requires only 2 bits of information to define it: 1 or 0. Therefore, the 6 by 8 letter *J* requires 48 bits of information to create it, 1 bit for each square.

DIGITAL ARTIST TOM MILLER created this image of a pirate using a graphics tablet in much the same way that a traditional painter would use brushes and paint.

- Edit with layers (separate pieces of art that can be combined later).
- Edit and convert between various color models.
- Apply various filters for special effects.
- Convert between various image formats.

ADOBE PHOTOSHOP®

Adobe Systems introduced one of the most popular of all raster graphic editors, Adobe Photoshop, in 1990. Adobe Photoshop has since become an industry standard against which all other similar programs are judged. Two brothers, Thomas and John Knoll, began developing Adobe Photoshop in 1987. They originally intended it to be a tool for working with images that were turned into digital form by a scanner, which was a rare and expensive device in those days.

Adobe Photoshop transformed the art of photo retouching and processing. The program's popularity, low cost, and ease of use brought about many advances in image editing. Procedures that had once taken hours or days by skilled photographers or artists—such as removing scratches and dirt or even replacing missing areas—became simple tasks that could be done by any amateur.

Adobe Photoshop also opened up the Internet to photographers and artists. It was one of the first programs that could prepare images for the World Wide Web. And with the introduction of the graphics tablet, artists and illustrators have been using software such as Adobe Photoshop and Corel® Paint Shop Pro® Photo X2 to create original works of art. Adobe Photoshop and similar programs are regularly used by professional illustrators, fine artists, comic-book artists, motion picture special-effects artists, and many others.

THE NEW PHOTOGRAPHY

Before computers, one of the very first creative uses of photography involved cutting and pasting bits and pieces from two or more original photos. Artists created entirely new images that could then be rephotographed. Artists also found ways to "print" photos right onto their canvases. They used the halftone process (a photo can be broken up into a pattern of tiny dots of different sizes) and combined it with silk screen (a method of transferring art to a

THE GRAPHICS TABLET

The graphics tablet is one of the most valuable tools used by the digital artist. It lets an artist work exactly as if drawing or painting with a pen or brush. The typical tablet is a flat, plastic pad with a matching pen. The pen acts as a mouse, doing everything a mouse can do and more.

Graphics tablets offer 256 levels of pressure sensitivity, so they can detect even the slightest actions. A grid of wires beneath the face of the tablet picks up a faint electronic signal from the pen point. This is analyzed to determine the position of the point, pen pressure, and other information, which is then sent to the computer. By changing the pressure of the pen on the tablet, the artist can create brushlike strokes, variable color fills or airbrush densities, and other unique effects.

A TYPICAL GRAPHICS TABLET.

By drawing on the surface of the tablet with the stylus—an electronic "pen"—artists can create freehand designs on the monitor, exactly as though they were painting with a brush or drawing with a pen or pencil.

surface by pressing ink through a screen made of silk). Artist Robert Rauschenberg perfected this technique.

Meanwhile, other artists found that the photograph itself could be altered creatively. For instance, by briefly exposing a photo to light during

IMAGE FORMATS

Digital images can be stored in a variety of formats, all bearing strange names such as TIFF or GIF. The formats all describe different ways of storing images, and each has its own special advantage. The major ones that most digital artists work with are:

JPEG (Joint Photographic Experts Group): JPEG image files are a lossy format. This means that because the image is compressed (reduced in size) each time it is saved, its quality degrades a little—in much the same way that a photocopy of a photocopy is not as good as the original. The compression, in most cases, does not harm the image unless the image is repeatedly edited and saved. Nearly all digital cameras have the option to save images in JPEG format. The JPEG format supports 8 bits per color—red, green, and blue, for a total of 24 bits—and makes somewhat small file sizes.

TIFF (tagged image file format): TIFF format normally saves 16 bits per color (red, green, and blue for a total of 48 bits) or 8 bits per color (red, green, and blue for a total of 24 bits). TIFF is a very flexible format that is popular with digital artists and photographers, especially those who are doing work that will appear in print. TIFF is the most widely accepted file standard in the printing industry. Some high-end digital cameras have the option to save images in the TIFF format. The TIFF image format, however, is not widely supported by Web browsers and should not be used for websites.

RAW: The RAW image format is a file option available on some digital cameras. It's called this because its files are not yet

developing, a bizarre effect called solarization would occur. Artists such as Man Ray (1890–1976) frequently used this technique. Other photo artists, such as Andre de Dienes (1913–1985), distorted images by reflecting a photo in warped mirrors and then photographing the reflected image.

processed and ready to use with a graphics program. The image must first be processed and switched to an RGB format such as TIFF or JPEG before it can be altered. It usually uses a lossless compression—that is, without any loss of detail or information—and produces file sizes much smaller than the TIFF format. Unfortunately, the RAW format is not standard in all cameras and some graphic programs and image editors may not accept it.

GIF (graphic interchange format): GIF is limited to an 8-bit palette, or 256 colors. This makes the GIF format suitable for storing graphics with few colors such as simple diagrams, shapes, and cartoonlike images. The GIF format supports animation and is widely used to provide image animation effects, especially on the Web. It also uses a lossless compression that is most effective when large areas have a single color and ineffective for detailed or dithered images.

PNG (portable network graphics): The PNG file format was developed as a successor to the GIF file format. The PNG file format supports true color—16 million colors. PNG works best when the image has large areas of uniform color. The lossless PNG format is best suited for editing pictures. (Lossy formats such as JPEG are best for distributing photographic images because of their smaller file size.)

BMP (bitmap): The main advantage of BMP files is their wide acceptance and use in Windows® programs. Their large size, however, makes them unsuitable for file transfer. Desktop backgrounds and images from scanners are usually stored as BMP files.

DIGITAL ART

Modern artists realized that they could use photography in brand-new ways with the computer. When companies introduced software such as Adobe Photoshop, all different kinds of artists—from traditional painters to photographers—found a middle ground. Once a photo was scanned into digital form, the possibilities were endless. It could be made part of a larger work of art, it could be altered creatively, or both.

Effects such as those used by Rauschenberg, de Dienes, and others, which had once taken hours or days to achieve, could be done in minutes. Since copies of digital images are identical to the original, artists could make changes without causing permanent damage to the original. When digital cameras became widely available, the creative use of photos became even easier. Artists could use digital photos right away on the computer.

ADOBE PHOTOSHOP AND SIMILAR PROGRAMS WERE originally developed for photo retouchers. Here a badly damaged photograph of Abraham Lincoln from the 1800s was restored by removing the flaws digitally.

AN EXAMPLE OF PHOTO MANIPULATION. THE ORIGINAL PHOTO
of a young woman *(left)* was altered to make it appear that her head had become a balloon.

Magazines, newspapers, and other publications found practical uses for editing software. For instance, editors could alter photos to better fit layouts and page designs. Unfortunately, editors could also alter photos to suit special needs. In the 1920s, publisher Bernarr Macfadden, with the invention of the composograph, pioneered the use of altered photos. It combined parts of several different photos to create a new one. A great many newspapers printed them without bothering to tell their readers that the images were pure fiction.

A modern case of this type of photo editing occurred in 1982. *National Geographic* editors digitally moved two Egyptian pyramids closer together so that they would fit better on the magazine cover. Although done without any intent to mislead the magazine's readers, the altered photo

THESE IMAGES SHOW JUST A FEW EXAMPLES OF THE HUNDREDS
of different effects digital artists can create with one photo using photo-editing software.

sparked a debate about using edited photos in journalism. People argued that the magazine had presented the photo as fact when it actually depicted something that did not exist. Other instances of altered photos have appeared in major magazines. Each time a heated debate erupts about the honesty of doing so—especially if the readers are not informed that the photo has been altered.

Many different image-editing software programs are available—such as Adobe Photoshop and Corel Paint Shop Pro Photo X2. But they all share some basic functions. Among these are:

- The ability to select all or part of an image
- The ability to use layers (Layers are similar to sheets of transparent plastic stacked on top of one another. Each layer can be individually positioned, altered, and blended with the layers below without affecting any of the elements on the other layers.)
- The ability to change the size and proportions of an image

- The ability to crop an image—that is, the ability to cut away unwanted portions of the top, bottom, and sides
- The ability to clean up an image by removing dust, scratches, and other imperfections
- The ability to change or adjust colors, contrast, light, and darkness
- The ability to cut and paste elements from one image to another

Such software is, of course, capable of many other functions. Different products offer distinct collections of tools.

PAINTING WITH PIXELS

Digital painters, on the other hand, do not work with computer-generated models or work with them very little. Instead, they treat the computer as their canvas and their mouse or tablet as a brush and palette, creating their digital painting directly on the computer. Traditional painting techniques such as watercolor, oils, charcoal, pen and ink, and so forth can be reproduced digitally.

The first digital painters worked more or less in traditional styles of painting. Soon they realized that the computer could provide techniques and styles that were unique to digital art. Some were combinations of traditional styles, while others required new definitions.

THIS DIGITAL PAINTING
by Kenji Bliss shows how much a digital
painting can resemble one painted with
traditional materials.

DIGITAL ART

USING LAYERS MAKES IT EASIER FOR DIGITAL

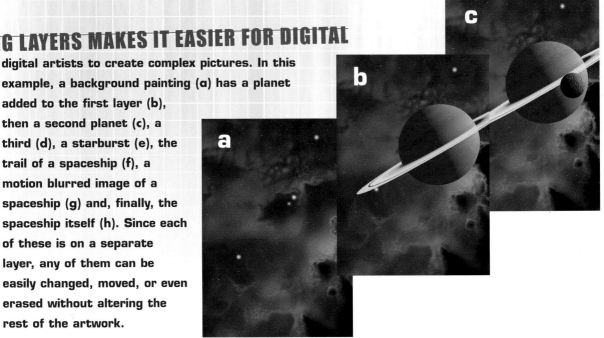

digital artists to create complex pictures. In this example, a background painting (a) has a planet added to the first layer (b), then a second planet (c), a third (d), a starburst (e), the trail of a spaceship (f), a motion blurred image of a spaceship (g) and, finally, the spaceship itself (h). Since each of these is on a separate layer, any of them can be easily changed, moved, or even erased without altering the rest of the artwork.

Artists were able to mix media that would have been difficult or impossible to do in reality. For instance, it is almost impossible to mix watercolors and oils. Artists could also include many different forms of digital media into their work. For example, text, video, animation, and audio can be made part of a single piece of art.

The computer offers artists other distinct advantages over traditional painting. For instance, artists can work in layers, keeping different elements of the painting separate. By doing this, artists can experiment without changing the entire painting. For example, an artist may want to add a figure to a scene but is unsure of exactly where it should go. By painting the figure on a separate layer, the artist can move it around until it is in exactly the desired place. And if the artist decides to omit the figure after all, it can simply be deleted.

The computer also allows artists to undo and redo certain elements. Artists can undo a mistake with a single keystroke—or something undone by mistake can be put back. This single ability is one of the greatest advantages digital artists have over artists working in traditional media. When a traditional artist makes a mistake, it might take hours or

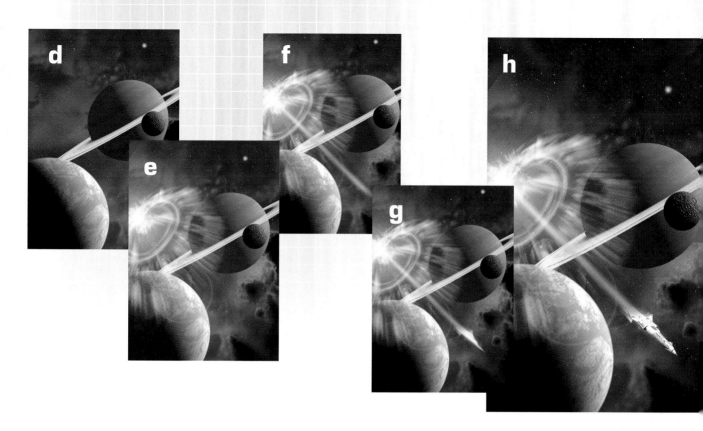

perhaps even days of hard work to undo. If a mistake is bad enough, a painting might have to be redone.

Digital artists have many tools not available to the traditional painter. Some of these include a palette with millions of colors; almost any size canvas or media; immediate access to tools such as pencils, airbrushes, spray cans, brushes, and sponges; as well as a variety of two-dimensional (2-D) and three-dimensional (3-D) effects. Digital painting also opened the way for unique collaborative efforts. Since it is easy to share digital artwork over the Internet, many artists can contribute to a single work of art.

One of the major drawbacks to painting digitally is that the tablet lacks the feel of traditional materials and tools. Drawing and painting with digital "oils," "watercolors," or "charcoal" all feel the same since they are all done with a stylus—a kind of pen—on the smooth plastic surface of a graphics tablet. To get around this, some artists will tape a sheet of paper on the surface of their tablet to get closer to the feel of drawing on paper.

DIGITAL ART

DIGITAL ARTIST ERIC SPRAY MADE THIS DIGITAL ILLUSTRATION
look as though it had been painted in acrylics or oils.

MODERN DIGITAL ART

Digital art can be purely computer generated, such as in fractals, or it can be taken from a scanned photograph. It can start with an image drawn with a mouse or graphics tablet, or it can be a combination of all these methods.

The widespread availability of photo-editing software, such as Adobe Photoshop, has resulted in tens of thousands of images that bear little or no resemblance to the originals. Certain artists specialize in using digital versions of the photographer's traditional filters, lenses, and enlargers. They create images impossible to attain by traditional means. They call themselves neographers (from Latin words meaning "new writers").

In addition to photos, artists can alter digital drawings and paintings in an endless variety of ways. They can combine, distort, and rework the images until they become something entirely new and original. Digital paintings and drawings can be found everywhere, from magazine illustrations to advertisements to graphic novels. These often imitate traditional painting techniques really well. Sometimes it is impossible to tell whether an artist created an illustration in oils, watercolors, acrylics, or pixels.

ART FOR DIFFERENT PURPOSES

Just as in traditional media, digital artists can be grouped into two broad categories: commercial artists and gallery artists. Commercial artists generally work for hire. Their paintings appear as magazine illustrations and book covers, in advertisements, on greeting cards, and more. Gallery artists work for themselves, selling their original works directly to collectors.

Many people try to make a hard distinction between "illustrations" and "fine art," but no definite line exists between the two. Some will suggest that illustrations are done by special order for a fee—that is, on commission. But most of the art done over the whole history of art was created for that very reason. Leonardo da Vinci painted *Last Supper* not as a work of art for its own sake but because a monastery paid him for it.

Other definitions for illustrations suggest that they are purely decorative or tell a story. But again, most of the art created over the past several thousand years was done for decoration or storytelling. It might be easy to define a drawing of a toaster in a catalog as purely commercial art and an abstract painting hanging in a museum as purely fine art. But a very broad gray area exists between the two. This is why you will sometimes find abstract paintings used in advertisements and paintings by famous illustrators—such as Norman Rockwell of the mid-1900s—hanging in museums.

DIGITAL FINE ART

The commercial art world has completely accepted digital art. But digital art still has not gained the full acceptance and respect given to "serious" art forms such as sculpture, painting, and drawing. Few galleries and museums take digital art seriously, and exhibitions are still somewhat rare.

This attitude is slowly changing, however. Digital fine art is no longer the novelty it once was. Digital tools have become a vital part of making art.

DIGITAL ART

As more artists produce works of art as good as those created with traditional media, people are taking digital art more seriously. A small number of museums are beginning to gather collections of important digital artwork.

Museums had been slow to collect digital art partly because of the impermanence of the media. The inks that artists use to create prints simply were not of archival quality. No museum wanted to acquire art that would fade away in a few years. Fortunately, researchers came up with new inks that will last decades if not centuries. The development of the giclee print got rid of many of the objections to digital art. This high-quality method of reproducing digital art features brilliant, permanent colors. Giclee prints can be made on a variety of materials other than paper. In fact, artists can have their digital pictures printed on real canvas if they wish. Modern digital prints are as permanent as any traditional etching or lithograph.

ERIC SPRAY'S DIGITAL FANTASY PAINTING AS TYPICAL OF THE high quality that has been attracting the attention of serious galleries and museums.

DIGITAL PAINTINGS SUCH AS THIS ONE BY KENJI BLISS
help bridge the gap between illustration and fine art.

As in any other art form, as many different approaches to digital art exist as do artists working in the media. Artworks range from the wildly abstract to images that are photographic in their realism—and every possible technique and style in between.

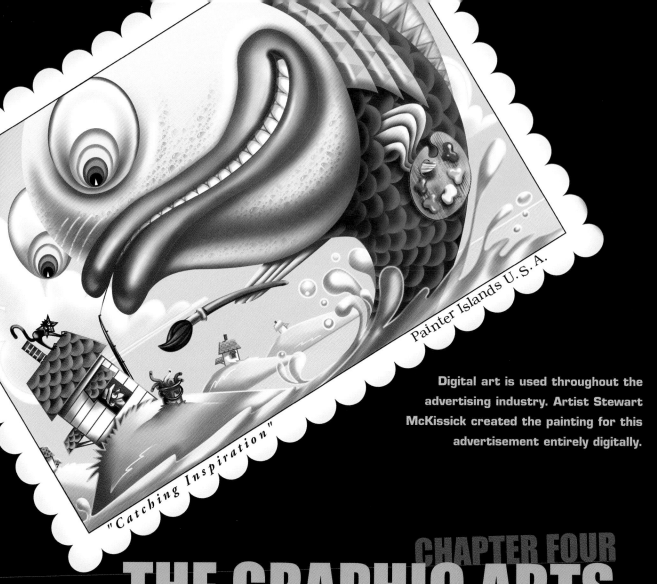

Painter Islands U.S.A.

"Catching Inspiration"

Digital art is used throughout the advertising industry. Artist Stewart McKissick created the painting for this advertisement entirely digitally.

CHAPTER FOUR
THE GRAPHIC ARTS

Digital art changed the field of graphic arts probably more than any other art form. Graphic art includes everything from book design to advertising layouts to illustrations. All of these have changed a great deal in just the past two decades.

At first, the use of digital art in the field of graphic arts wasn't promising. Soon after the introduction of Adobe Photoshop, many budding book cover designers found the software's ability to combine and blend many images together in elaborate collages. The result was often murky, colorless, and confusing. And it all tended to look very much alike. Art like this became so common that many art directors refused to accept any art that had been done with Adobe Photoshop, good or bad.

Ultimately, art directors were put off by the low quality of digital illustration, regardless of the software used to create it. But they didn't have a problem with the media itself. The poor artwork resulted from the media being used by unskilled artists. However, as more skillful artists began using digital media, the quality of digital art improved. It became more acceptable to the art directors, editors, and designers of books and magazines. Digital art can be found almost everywhere.

MAGAZINE, BOOK DESIGN, AND ADVERTISING

Digital art has drastically changed the field of book and magazine design. What had once been a time-consuming and costly process involving many

THIS ADVERTISING ART BY STEWART MCKISSICK LOOKS AS IF it were created with pen and ink. It would have been time consuming to create with such traditional methods.

WORDS FROM AN EXPERT

I knew the tide had turned in favor of digital artwork over traditional media when while giving a visitor a tour of the offices of *Scientific American* magazine, I realized all of the artwork hanging on our walls was over five years old. Normally we'd hang a new original piece of art, courtesy of the artist, every few months after it had been published. Over time, we've received fewer and fewer pieces completed in traditional media. The last piece of traditional media artwork we received was six months ago. We had to remember how to process it.

Traditional media certainly isn't "dead." Many pieces are still done with oil, color pencil, acrylic, and other media, but at some point they are scanned and finished in the computer. This allows the artist to make more quickly the inevitable changes that are all too common with scientific illustration. The pressure from publishers and editors on artists to make quick and numerous changes may be the single biggest reason many scientific illustrators have switched from traditional to digital media.

Digital tools such as undo and layering allow artists to expedite corrections and alterations. Additionally, these tools foster creative experimentation by allowing the artists to say "what if . . ." without the penalty of reconstruction of the image. It is of little wonder, then, that the vast majority of commercial artists are now using digital media to create most if not all of their work.

If there is a problem with digital art (and there is), it is that many artists become infatuated with the many bells and whistles that are available on most graphic programs. They get lost in the morass of drop shadows, custom brushes, special effects and filters, and other "instant art" menu selections, while ignoring the basic skills they learned to become an artist. Worse still, people with no art or graphics training are using the computer and producing bad artwork. But that is the bad news. The good news is that the maturation, evolution, and sophistication of graphics software, combined with the mastery of that software by serious artists and illustrators, have led to a wealth of excellent digitally created artwork.

As the publishing industry's reliance on digital imagery increases, so will the pressure on artists to increase their knowledge of the new media. As digital media has taken time to mature, so will these new disciplines. Artists who are swift to master the world of digital art will find plenty of work. We await their arrival.

—Ed Bell, art director, *Scientific American* magazine

skilled people can be achieved in minutes by a single person. With computers, even the smallest publication working on the tightest budget can achieve effects once reserved to the biggest magazines and book publishers. Moreover, computers and computer graphics let designers create effects that would have been impossible to do by hand.

The biggest impact has been how publishers have streamlined the entire process of book and magazine design. The publisher of this book that you are reading created it entirely by using computers. The words were written, edited, and set digitally. The artwork and photos were all digitized and in many cases created digitally in the first place. The book designer added decorative elements and colors digitally and combined everything into a single file on a computer before sending it to the printer. All of this is done by several people, whereas less than twenty years ago, it may have taken dozens.

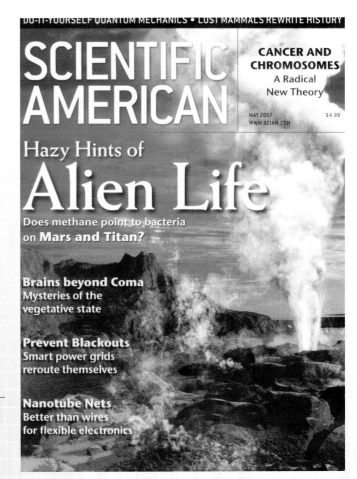

THE ILLUSTRATION FOR THIS magazine cover as well as the design and typography were all created digitally.

In addition, designers and other artists can be creative in many new ways. Artwork does not have to be either wholly digital or wholly painted. Hybrid works of art combine the best features of traditional painting techniques and digital media. For instance, an artist may do a painting in oils, acrylics, or watercolors; scan the painting; and then complete it using computer software.

Typography—the art of designing with typefaces and words—provides another example of the creative freedom of digital art. In the past, making fancy type required the work of an expert, who would do all the work entirely by hand. With computers, designers can achieve fantastic effects with type in a matter of minutes. They can distort type so that it looks as though it were made of metal or glass or any other material. Designers can make type appear three-dimensional or as though it were melting or on fire—anything that the magazine or book design requires.

DIGITAL ART

BEFORE THE ADVENT OF DIGITAL ART, DESIGNERS WERE VERY limited in what they could do with type. If they needed something beyond the standard type available (such as the example at the top), a special artist would have to do it by hand. With computers, however, designers can create special effects quickly and easily. The bottom example was done in one minute using only half a dozen basic controls in Adobe Photoshop.

THEN AND NOW

A typical magazine ad provides a perfect example of how the field has changed. Up until the last two decades of the twentieth century, editors put together magazine ads using a technique called cut and paste. Type, photos, art, and every other element that would appear on the printed page had to be cut and pasted by hand onto a large sheet of special art board. Each layer of art was placed on a separate board.

Next, a photoengraver prepared the ad by taking each layer of art and making a photographic negative of it. The negatives would then be combined into a single one from which the final product could be printed. The entire process was very complex, time consuming, expensive, and required the efforts of several skilled people and special materials.

THIS ADVERTISING PIECE

by Stewart McKissick shows how digital art is particularly useful for creating decorative shapes with simple, bright colors.

The computer, on the other hand, let the designer do almost all of this work at a desktop. This did away with the process of photographing each piece of art. So a process that had once required the efforts of several skilled people as well as hours or even days of time and costly materials could be done in a few hours or even minutes by a single person. Also, designers could create effects that are difficult to do the old way or perhaps even simply impossible. Whole new realms of creativity opened up for the designer.

ONE OF THE ADVANTAGES OF DIGITAL ART IS THE ABILITY TO

combine many different media and techniques into a single image. This advertisement created by Tom Miller for a new toy combines three-dimensional modeling, digital painting, and digital photography.

Digital art has influenced the field of advertising more than any other industry, mostly because advertising uses so many different forms of digital art. Everything from magazine ads to television commercials have benefited from digital imagery. Artists creating magazine and newspaper ads have all the same creative freedom that magazine and book designers have. Television commercials have especially benefited from digital art since they can feature great special effects once reserved for big-budget motion pictures.

DESIGNING THIS BOOK

I used Adobe Photoshop together with page layout software (Adobe inDesign©) to create this book. Of course, creative vision is necessary for the book design process, but having powerful software—along with the ability to use it—is an invaluable tool.

One of the first steps in creating the book you are reading (the process is not always the same for every book) was to design the cover. The fact that this book is about digital art opened up a world of options for the graphics on the front cover. But it had to be cool so people would want to pick it up.

After we searched for the perfect image, I used Photoshop to incorporate all the necessary elements. The picture on the front is attention grabbing, so I wanted the title to look the same. I used a basic font because if I chose a more decorative one it would have competed with the image—all elements should work together. The colors I chose were picked up from the image itself but intensified a bit to really stand out from the dark background.

Working on the interior of the book is the same kind of process. This is where the page layout program comes in handy. Designers generally want to keep a consistent look throughout their projects, although the opposite can come in handy as well. For instance, no angles are used on the outside of the book, but I chose to use an angle on the contents page as well as various elements throughout. It contrasts all the strong, straight lines in the book. I intended it to add movement and keep the design from being boring. Using contrast is a great way to make something stand out whether it is with color or placement.

I carried the colors throughout and also brought in the font used on the cover. I also had to choose a few other fonts. I chose the font for the text because it's easy to read. I chose the subhead, caption, and sidebar fonts—along with the grid backgrounds—with the digital art "feel" in mind. It's amazing how design elements such as fonts and colors can work together to create a feel or mood without the reader being consciously aware of it. Obviously designers choose different looks for different audiences.

A lot more thought goes into the treatment and placement of elements than one might think—everything should be intentional. If you ask any designer why an object in any of their projects is placed where it is, they will have an answer—at least a good designer will.

—Amelia LeBarron, book designer, Lerner Publishing Group, Inc.

DIGITAL ART

COMIC BOOKS AND GRAPHIC NOVELS

Comic-book artists also realized the potential of digital art. Before computers, adding color to comic books was difficult and not always satisfactory. Because so much work was involved, comic-book artists rarely ever colored their own books. Instead, they simply indicated the colors on a tissue overlay and left the rest up to a colorist. Artists would indicate the colors with codes such as M50Y50 for 50 percent magenta and 50 percent yellow. Some comic-book artists simply wrote "pale blue" or "yellow" and hoped for the best.

This method resulted in flat areas of color with very sharp, hard edges. Sometimes colorists tried to avoid this by painting directly on the overlays. By using different tones of gray, they made soft changes in color tones as well as created soft edges to the colors. They achieved surprisingly subtle color blends and shading. The results were beautiful, but the process was time consuming and required a talented artist.

COMIC-BOOK ARTIST
Nate Piekos explains the steps involved in creating his digital comic-book cover.

1 Here we have the finished inks. I ended up using a lot of white acrylic paint to fix the areas where I was a bit overzealous with the brickwork. I also added that white line that goes around Barry and the hand to better separate the foreground from the background.

2 It took about three hours to digitally color this cover. I "washed out" the background a bit to better separate it from the foreground. If you're really interested in how I computer color my art, visit RealmOfAtland.com and read the articles in the Bits & Pieces section.

3 The last step is to add the cover copy. I keep a template of the logo, banner, and publisher's mark on my hard drive so that I can quickly layer the art behind it and change the colors to complement the artwork. And with that, another cover is finished!

THESE ARE PAGES FROM AN ONLINE DIGITAL COMIC

book called *Dewclaw* by artist Matt Johnson. Johnson drew and colored the art using vector graphics so it can be enlarged as much as necessary without losing any detail.

THIS PAGE FROM A COMIC BOOK WAS DRAWN
and colored digitally by artist **Nate Piekos.**

Comic-book artists and publishers began using computers to color their books in the mid-1980s. Software such as Adobe Photoshop and Adobe Illustrator sped up the process of coloring comics. It also let artists achieve very artistic, even painterly effects. Comic-book artists could also work much more closely with their colorist—or even do the coloring themselves.

Artists can use collages, photos, and many other creative techniques with the computer. Comic-book artists can even draw with the computer by using a graphics tablet instead of the traditional pen or brush.

Graphic novels—longer comic books that tell a long, complex story—have particularly benefited from digital artwork. They are typically printed on better paper, which allows for better coloring than regular comic books. Oddly enough, many comic-book artists who liked the look of old-fashioned comics are re-creating the bright, flat process colors through computer graphics.

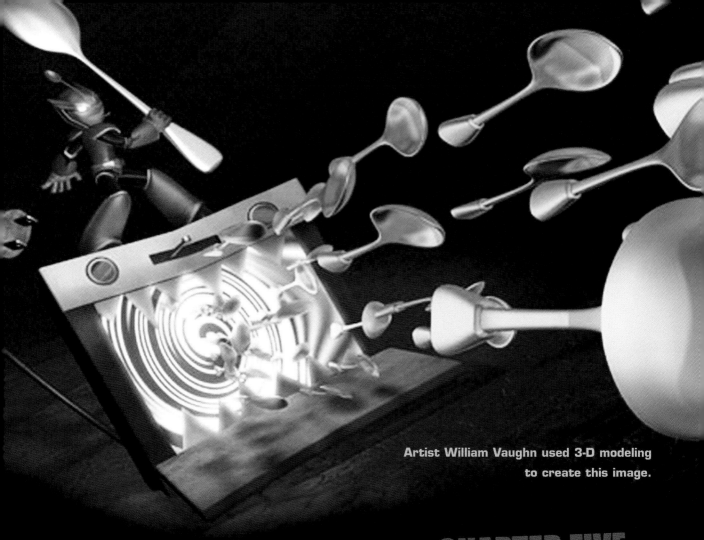

Artist William Vaughn used 3-D modeling to create this image.

CHAPTER FIVE

3-D MODELING

The earliest computer art was two-dimensional, such as drawings or paintings on paper or canvas. They were flat and could only be viewed from one direction. You could not take a drawing of a person and turn it around to see their side or back. If artists didn't like the lighting on a subject, they would have to do the digital painting over again. Computer artists took the next step from flat two-dimensional computer drawings by creating views of objects in three dimensions.

A 3-D model is usually displayed as a 2-D image on a computer monitor. Artists can use the computer's controls to move the model any way they like, so they can view it from any direction. A 3-D model can be created entirely from the imagination of an artist. The movie industry uses 3-D models of imaginary characters and objects for films and special effects. The video game industry uses them in computer and video games.

But 3-D models can also be used to re-create objects in the real world. Medical researchers and doctors, for instance, create detailed models of internal organs. Sometimes they create these from 3-D information gathered from living human beings using machines such as CAT scanners. Meteorologists create realistic models of storms and weather systems. Chemists and physicists create models of atomic structures and molecular compounds, while geologists re-create details of Earth that lie deep underground. Architects use 3-D models to show proposed buildings and landscapes. Engineers use them to test and demonstrate new devices, vehicles, and structures.

MODELING

Three-dimensional modeling consists mostly of building complex shapes from very simple ones (primitives), such as cylinders, cones, and spheres. A 3-D model by itself is not something you can see or hold in your hand. Instead, it is a purely mathematical construction that can be displayed in many ways, including its raw mathematical form—that is, as a series of numbers. It can be a wire frame model, which is a simple version of the model that shows the basic shapes in the form of lines. No shading, color, or textures exist. Or artists can shade the model in a variety of ways. By including appropriate light, shadow, and color, artists can make the model appear photographically realistic.

Computer artists create models with programs made specifically for that purpose, such as 3ds Max®, Rhinoceros®, or Autodesk Maya®. In some cases, artists build models using several different programs. Each performs its own special function. For instance, one program creates the basic model, while another adds light and shadow.

Most 3-D models for general viewing are covered with a texture. A texture is really nothing more than a graphic image, such as a photo, that

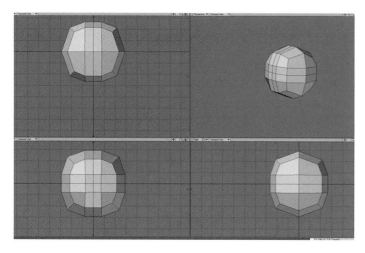

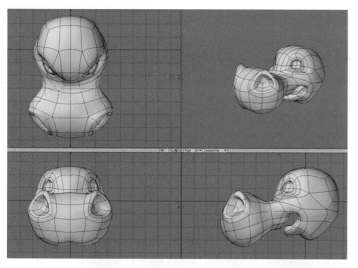

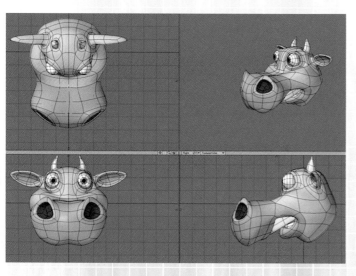

artists place over the surface of the model like a form-fitting skin. It gives the model more detail than a simple flat color would, making it look more realistic. A 3-D model of an animal or person, for example, looks much more realistic with skin, clothing, scales, or fur than it would as a simple wire frame model. Lining up the texture to specific spots on the 3-D model so that the texture fits the model correctly is called texture mapping.

Modelers can create soft models, such as clouds, dust, and flame, by using particle systems. Particle systems are simply a mass of 3-D shapes that define the overall shape of the image. For instance, if a modeler wants to make a trail of smoke from an airplane, he will create a collection of small spheres, each of which follows a path from the plane. These spheres can have soft edges and contain different types of effects that look like smoke, fog, or flame.

THIS SERIES OF IMAGES

from digital animator William Vaughn demonstrates some of the steps in creating a character from basic geometric shapes.

THE FLAMES IN THIS IMAGE BY DIGITAL ANIMATOR
William Vaughn were created using particle systems.

The smaller these spheres are, the more realistic the effect will be. But the smaller sizes take a very long time for a computer to process, which can be very costly. This is why you will often be able to tell if smoke is computer generated. It will look speckled or look as though it were made of many soft, cottonlike balls, because you can see the individual particles.

Artists can make images even more realistic by using special techniques such as bump mapping. Bump maps create the illusion of three-dimensional textures. Artists create special texture maps for this purpose. They paint a pattern of light and dark areas on what will eventually be the 3-D texture. The computer reads anything that is light colored as being high and anything dark colored as being low. The lighter a shape is, the higher its "bump" will be. The darker it is, the deeper it will appear.

3-D MODELING

DIGITAL ART

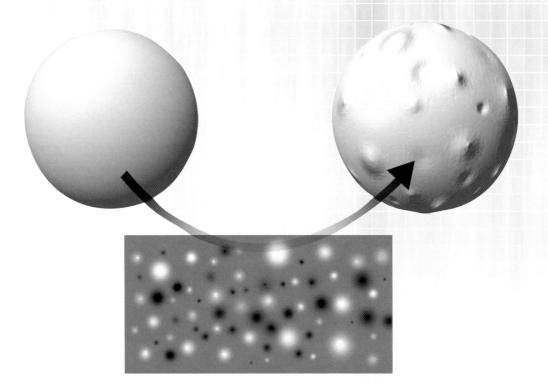

BUMP MAPS ARE USED TO CREATE THE APPEARANCE OF

texture on digital models. Here a smooth sphere is made to appear as though it has pits and craters by applying the bump map below it. The computer interprets light areas as raised and dark areas as lowered. The actual shape of the underlying sphere has not been changed.

Bump maps have only limited use. The textures are not truly three-dimensional since they don't actually change the shape of the model. A displacement map, however, will actually distort the shape of the model itself. This results in much more realistic textures but takes much longer for the computer to process.

REFINING THE MODEL

Once modelers create the basic model, artists can refine it further, depending on the level of detail and realism needed. A cartoonlike human, for instance, needs much less detail and realism than a model meant to look like a real person. Often these details are added by different artists, each specializing in certain areas.

Texture artists can add all sorts of properties to the surface of the model, such as shading, color, glows, reflections, and so on. They can make the model smooth or rough, they can add textures and bump maps, and they can make the model opaque or transparent. In short, the modeler creates a solid sphere, while the texture artists make it a bowling ball, a crystal ball, or the planet Earth.

The lighting of a model is a specialty that is often carried out by an individual artist. Lighting is important to the quality of the finished work. Lighting effects contribute greatly to the mood and emotional response of a scene. As such, it can be difficult to master (this is well known to photographers and theatrical lighting technicians). To make the most realistic models possible, digital artists have to include realistic lighting.

Light is reflected when it bounces off a surface, such as a shiny piece of metal. On the other hand, light is refracted when it passes through an object, such as a lens or glass of water. When light does this, it changes

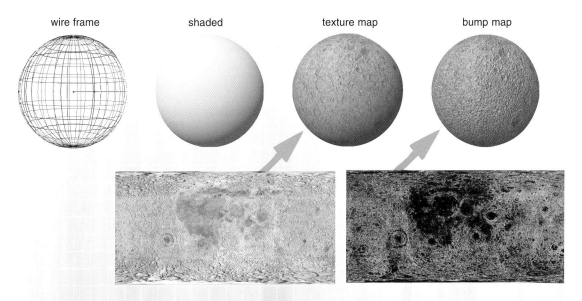

wire frame   shaded   texture map   bump map

TO CREATE AN IMAGE OF A PLANET, THE DIGITAL ARTIST FIRST created a simple sphere in wire frame mode *(upper left)*. The artist then covered it with a surface and added lighting. He also applied a texture *(lower left)*—in this case a map of the Moon—to the sphere. Next, he added a bump map *(lower right)*. The computer interpreted the light areas as being high and the dark as being low, resulting in a realistic 3-D texture for the Moon.

3-D MODELING

direction, intensity, and sometimes color. The way that light is reflected and refracted helps define the shapes of objects. It also helps define what those objects are made of.

An important concept in lighting is the refractive index. This indicates how much a certain material will bend light passing through it. Diamonds, for instance, have a much higher refractive index than glass. This high index means that diamonds bend light more, which is why they sparkle.

Creating reflected and refracted light uses a lot of computing power. The computer must calculate the paths of millions upon millions of individual rays of light as they pass through and bounce off every object in a scene.

RENDERING

The final process of creating the actual 3-D image or animation from all of its parts is called rendering. Rendering combines everything the artists have done—the model itself, textures, lighting, and so on, as well as the scene around the model—into a single image. This can be compared to taking a photo or shooting a scene in a film after the sets have been built and the actors posed. Rendering is an entirely automatic process that the computer carries out. When artists are ready, they direct the computer to begin the rendering process. The artist has nothing else to do until the computer is finished.

Rendering for interactive media such as video games is calculated and displayed in actual time, at rates of about 20 to 120 frames per second. That is, the computer produces a new scene—or "frame"—20 to 120 times every second. This is one of the reasons why the characters in games are not as realistic as they are in movies and why the animation is not as smooth or natural. It's just not possible (at the moment anyway) to create detailed, high-resolution renderings that quickly.

Animation for motion pictures or video, on the other hand, is rendered much more slowly. Instead of rendering twenty or more frames every second, a computer might take anywhere from several minutes to several hours to render a single frame for a movie. Sometimes it could take even a day or longer if the scene is complex enough. Computer programmers place no limits on the time or power the computer takes to render a frame. So digital artists can obtain great detail and realism.

Computer artists store the rendered frames on a hard disk. Later, they can transfer the frames to other media such as motion picture film. When moviemakers project each of these individually rendered frames at twenty-four frames a second, they create the illusion of motion.

The 3-D digital artist can render a scene in several ways. The choice depends more or less on the art's final purpose. Some of the techniques are better suited for photo-realistic renderings, while others are preferred for the real-time rendering in video games. The techniques range from the simplicity of wire frame rendering to more advanced techniques such as ray tracing and radiosity.

DIGITAL ARTIST WILLIAM VAUGHN USED RAY TRACING AND radiosity to create the realistic lighting, reflections, and shadows in this illustration.

Ray tracing re-creates the paths of individual rays of light as they interact with different surfaces. Scientists originally designed it for optical systems, such as camera lenses, microscopes, telescopes, and binoculars. Radiosity more closely imitates the way light works in the real world. For instance, it can accurately re-create how colors will

SPECIAL TECHNIQUES

Rendering software can reproduce visual effects such as lens flares, depth of field, or motion blur. We see all these effects in photos, movies, and nature—whether we are aware of them or not. Lens flares, for instance, happen when light is reflected within and between the lenses in a camera. Depth of field occurs when objects too near or too far from the camera or eye are not in focus. (If you hold a finger a foot or so from your eyes and focus on it, objects in the distance will be out of focus). Motion blur happens when the subject in a photo moves while the shutter is open. If artists add motion blur to a 3-D model, it will look as if the model was photographed while in motion. Effects such as these can add greatly to the realism of a scene.

Digital artists developed special techniques to re-create other naturally occurring effects, such as the interaction of light with different forms of matter. Examples of such techniques

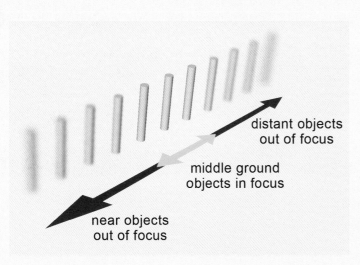

distant objects
out of focus

middle ground
objects in focus

near objects
out of focus

DEPTH OF FIELD REFERS TO THE AREA a camera lens can keep in sharp focus. Objects too near the lens will be out of focus and so will objects that are too far away. Since cameras and the human eye both work this way, digital artists can make their scenes look more realistic by re-creating this effect in their

affect an object, creating more realistic colors, shadows, and reflections.

In real-time rendering, the artist's goal is to show as much information as the eye can process in the time it takes to project one frame: about one-thirtieth of a second. The goal is obviously speed rather than photo-realism. Artists have been achieving greater realism as computer technology improves.

include particle systems (to re-create rain, smoke, or fire) and volumetric sampling (to re-create fog, dust, and other atmospheric effects). Other techniques include caustics (to re-create light on uneven light-refracting surfaces, such as the light ripples on the bottom of a swimming pool) and subsurface scattering (to re-create light reflecting inside solid, translucent objects such as human skin).

DIGITAL ANIMATOR WILLIAM VAUGHN used depth of field and motion blur in this frame from one of his animated films. These techniques give the viewer a sense of motion and depth.

These techniques are expensive to render. And the more of them artists use in a scene, the longer the rendering will take. Although computer processing power has increased rapidly over the years, film studios that produce digital animation use many computers at once (called a render farm). This shortens the amount of time it takes to create a sequence on film.

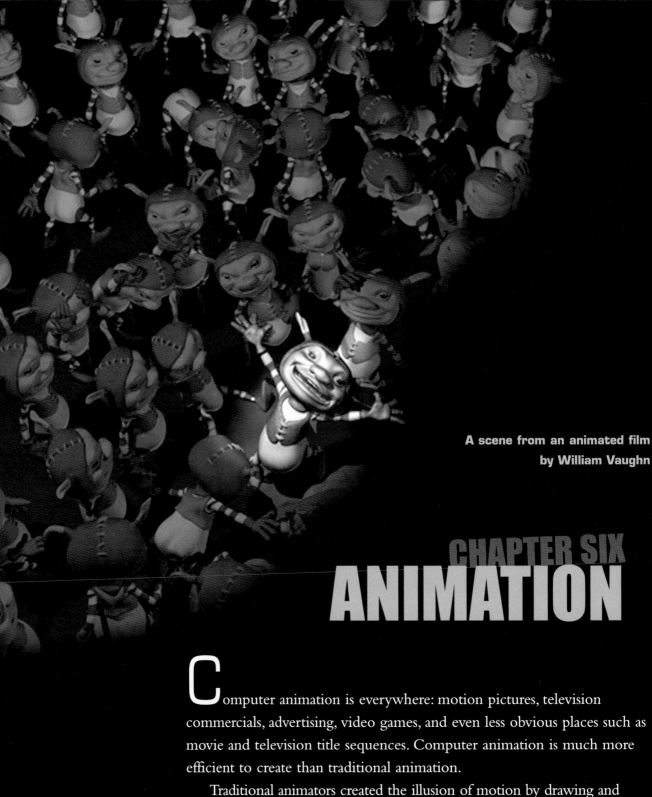

A scene from an animated film
by William Vaughn

CHAPTER SIX

ANIMATION

Computer animation is everywhere: motion pictures, television commercials, advertising, video games, and even less obvious places such as movie and television title sequences. Computer animation is much more efficient to create than traditional animation.

Traditional animators created the illusion of motion by drawing and coloring thousands of individual cels. Each cel would then be photographed as a frame of film. When animators ran the film through a projector, the drawings appeared to be moving. This was a long and difficult process.

Motion picture film runs at twenty-four frames a second. Animators must create twenty-four individual drawings for every second of film. A typical Bugs Bunny or Mickey Mouse cartoon runs for about seven minutes—that's 10,080 separate cels that had to be created! Some cartoon producers saved time and money by using fewer frames per second, but they lost smooth movement. The jerky effect you see in many Japanese cartoons is a result of this.

COMPUTER ANIMATION

Computer animation works exactly the same way as traditional animation. An individual still image is created for every frame of film. However, instead of an artist having to draw and color every picture by hand, the computer does it automatically. The computer does this in much the same way as traditional cel animation.

In cel animation, a lead animator created the key movements of a character—the beginning and end of movement and any important changes of movement or direction in between. For example, the lead animator might only create a drawing of a character with its hand on a cup and another drawing of the character holding the cup to its mouth. These drawings would then be handed over to a team of in-betweeners (often shortened to tweeners). The in-betweeners filled in the dozens or hundreds of frames in between the key movements set by the lead animator.

Computer animation works in a similar way. The computer animator creates a character and then sets up certain key points in the character's movement. The computer then takes the character through all the movements in between the key points.

Animating 2-D images is very similar to animating the flat drawings of a painted cel. Animating 3-D images is similar in many ways but a great deal more complex. Just as in 2-D animation, the computer doesn't actually create a moving image. Instead, it makes a great many individual still pictures. To animate a racing car, for instance, the computer simply makes hundreds of different images of the car, each from a slightly different angle. Moviemakers put the images onto film and run them through a projector, which creates the illusion of motion.

ANIMATOR WILLIAM VAUGHN USED SIMPLE SHAPES AND basic colors to create the characters and setting in this animated scene.

The difficult part of 3-D animation lies in the images themselves. The images are typically much more complex than ordinary 2-D animation. They involve light and shadow, reflections, textures, and many other details that computers have to render for every single frame of film. As the car moves, the lighting changes on its surface and the shadow it casts on the ground changes as does shadows cast on the car by the objects it passes. Reflections on the car and its windows also change. Computers must calculate and render all these effects.

CREATING DIGITAL CHARACTERS

Digital animators create their characters in a number of ways. They can create a model from scratch by building it in the computer using 3-D software. This is most often done when the model is of an inanimate object, such as a building or spacecraft. They can also create a model from an actual 3-D object. This is most often done when the model is of an animal or human being.

To do this, sculptors create an actual model of the subject. They mark points on the surface of the model and draw lines connecting them. This divides the surface into a spiderweb-like grid. They place more points where the most complex animation is to take place and fewer points where not much movement occurs. For instance, the areas around mouths and eyes need much more detailed animation than other areas.

THIS IMAGE SHOWS TWO STAGES IN THE CREATION OF A digitally animated character. In the image on the right, the artist has added details, textures, and color to the basic, early rendering on the left.

Animators then record the position of each of these points in 3-D space by using a special pen. Since the computer recognizes the location of the pen, the surface grid can be digitized. Animators actually build a virtual model in the computer's memory. Some animators may instead choose to use a device called a cyberscanner. This device uses laser beams to measure the 3-D position of thousands of points. Cyberscanners can create digital models of very complex objects—such as the human body—accurately and very quickly.

Once animators create models, they begin adding the details. To copy the movements of a living creature—even an imaginary one such as Gollum in *Lord of the Rings* (2002) or the fish in *Finding Nemo* (2003)—the model needs a skeleton. The skeleton is a central framework that affects the shape or movements of the object. The movement of the skeleton automatically affects corresponding portions of the model. So, moving one part of the skeleton will automatically move adjoining parts. A digital skeleton allows different parts of the body to move in realistic relationship to one another.

Objects such as humans and animals are the most difficult and require the most rendering time since they must appear realistic. Unlike monsters or aliens, everyone knows what a human being looks like and, consciously or not, is very aware of small errors in appearance and especially movement. This forces animators to take great care in animating people since even the slightest error will ruin the illusion of reality.

To animate humans and animals realistically, animators give them "muscles"

INVERSE KINEMATICS

A very important distinction exists between the way models were once animated by hand and the way they are animated by computer. In an old movie such as *King Kong* (1933), the animator had to move Kong's shoulder, arm, elbow, and hand separately to move Kong's entire arm. The animator had to keep track of all the different movements and could often only create a few seconds of film every day.

Modern computer modelers use a technique called inverse kinematics (IK). To create a realistic movement of a creature's arm, they only need to grab the hand and move it where they want it to go. All the other connected body parts will follow its lead. The effect is like that of a puppeteer moving a marionette's hand and the arm and body following suit. Inverse kinematics not only saves a lot of time and effort but also creates extremely realistic movements.

EXPERIMENT WITH DIGITAL ANIMATION

If you have a paint program (such as Adobe Photoshop) and an animation program (many free programs are available online, such as Tapptoons), you can make an animated movie. Using the painting or drawing program, create a series of simple pictures. Each one should be the same height and width. Number each image file as you do it (for example: 01, 02, 03, and so on), and save them in the format (.gif or .bmp) recommended by the animation program. Each picture will be a separate frame in your animation.

When you are finished, export all the images into the animation program. The program will allow you to make some fine adjustments, such as the time each frame will be displayed. You can use as many or as few drawings as you like. Often only two or three different drawings are enough to suggest motion. Just as in a professional animated film, though, the more frames you create, the smoother and more realistic the results will be. Instead of animating hand-drawn characters, commercially available programs such as Poser and Strata 3D CX let you create and animate realistic 3-D human figures and objects.

and "skin." Muscles are little more than shapes attached to the skeleton that stretch and bulge like real muscles when the figure moves. When the digital skin is applied, the movement of the muscles will be visible beneath it, creating a very lifelike appearance. Finally, animators apply color and textures to the skin.

When animators move one part of the figure's body, all the other parts will move in proportion just as they would in nature. By moving the bones and joints and letting the overlying layers follow suit, animators can create very realistic movements. The dinosaurs in *Jurassic Park* (1993) were one of the first demonstrations of this technique. The dinosaurs' skin and muscles moved realistically over their internal skeletons. Animators can also give models specific controls to make animation easier. For instance, controls for facial expression and mouth shapes (called phonemes) allow animators to coordinate lip movement with spoken words.

MOTION CAPTURE

To achieve the most realistic movements possible, especially when animating a human being, some digital animators will "trace" the movements of an actor. They do this often when creating computer sports games. A real-life sports hero will have a digital counterpart who must move just like the real person.

TO CAPTURE THE MOTION OF A MOVING FIGURE, THE ACTOR

is dressed entirely in black with reflective lines and spots attached to the costume *(above)*. When the actor's movements are videotaped and passed through a computer, the person's motion can be converted to a form that is then copied by an animated character *(below)*.

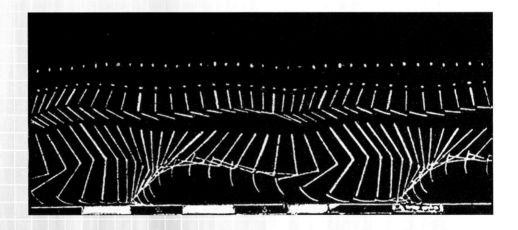

To digitize the movements of a human being, animators use a technique called motion capture. They dress a person in black from head to foot. Then they attach Ping-Pong balls to all the key points of the body: head, shoulders, elbows, knees, and so forth. The balls are coated with a reflective material. Digital motion picture cameras surround the person at precisely measured fixed positions. The person then goes through the motions of the animated character. The computer can combine the data into a single 3-D image that looks something like a white stick figure against a black background.

With this data, digital artists can look at the movement from any angle, finally choosing the one they want to use. They use the computer model as the basis for creating the animated character, which will move exactly as the actor did. The technique results in particularly realistic motions, such as those of Gollum in *Lord of the Rings*, the skeletal pirates in *Pirates of the Caribbean* (2003), and many of the human characters in *The Polar Express* (2004).

Rotoscoping is a technique distantly related to motion capture. Animators originally developed it for traditional cel animation to show more realistic movements of humans and animals. In rotoscoping, filmmakers shoot footage of an actor in motion. Rotoscope artists then trace this footage frame by frame. The result is a cartoon character that moves very realistically. Animators used a digital form of rotoscoping in the film *A Scanner Darkly* (2006). Using a special program called Rotoshop, digital animators made live-action footage of actors look like hand-drawn animation.

In this scene from an experimental
science fiction film, the model
spacecraft were combined with the
background scene digitally.

MOTION PICTURE SPECIAL EFFECTS

The first motion picture to use computer-generated imagery (CGI) was
TRON (1982)—although some early digital elements were used to a
limited degree in *Westworld* (1973) and *Futureworld* (1976). With much of
its action taking place in an imaginary world set within a computer,
TRON's animation did not have to look very realistic, and it didn't.

In the same year, Paramount released *Star Trek II: The Wrath of Khan*
(1982). It featured a single, brief computer-generated sequence in which
an entire planet is created in just a few seconds, from barren rock to lush

vegetation, lakes, and cloudy skies. While lasting only a few seconds on film, the so-called Genesis effect was much more realistic than anything filmmakers attempted in *TRON*.

The success of the effect led to *The Last Starfighter* (1984). This movie featured a great deal of computer-generated imagery. Most notably, the filmmakers used computer-generated models of spacecraft instead of traditionally built ones, such as those in *2001: A Space Odyssey* (1968) or *Star Wars* (1977). CGI spacecraft could do things that would be difficult or impossible to achieve with a model. But they did not look nearly as convincing, with flat, plasticlike surfaces and little or no texture.

The first computer-generated movie character was the "stained glass knight" featured in *Young Sherlock Holmes* (1985). But directors were still wary of computer-generated special effects until the early 1990s, when director Steven Spielberg began working on *Jurassic Park*. At first Spielberg intended to create the dinosaurs in the film through a combination of

JURASSIC PARK WAS THE FIRST MOTION PICTURE TO MAKE extensive use of digitally animated creatures. The level of realism the digital artists achieved set a high standard for later films.

traditional 3-D animation and animatronics (full-size mechanized models). But when animator Phil Tippett tested some computer-generated dinosaurs, he convinced Spielberg to make the majority of the dinosaur effects digitally.

Spielberg's decision affected the entire course of the special-effects industry. *Jurassic Park* proved that computer-generated effects were capable of creating astonishingly realistic images. It also proved that digital animators could convincingly re-create living creatures as well. The dinosaurs of *Jurassic Park* genuinely seemed to be living, breathing animals. (In fact, the film's special-effects team won the 1993 Academy Award for Visual Effects.)

HOW IT WORKS

Motion picture film is made up of a long strip of transparent plastic covered with a thin coating of light-sensitive material. This material is made up of microscopic particles. If the picture is enlarged enough, these particles become visible as a random pattern of speckles. These speckles are called the film's grain.

The creation of a picture is a chemical process that changes the particles that make up the grain. Once the picture is formed, it is permanent and little can be done to change it. A digital image is entirely different. It is composed of pixels. The big difference between pixels and film grain is that the pixel is not permanent. It can be any color or shade that the computer artist wants to make it. This is because the pixel is not a chemically changed particle. It is a number in a computer. All the computer artist has to do is change the numbers on the pixels.

Motion pictures are recorded on ordinary film. Filmmakers can then digitize the film frame by frame and store it in a computer. This is the same process by which you can turn a photograph into a digital image using a scanner. Once a computer technician digitizes a movie—or those parts of a movie that need special effects—the digital effects artist can change it in exactly the same way you can change a scanned photograph. They can add matte paintings, computer-generated 3-D objects, and effects animation. They can also make subtle changes to color and many other adjustments.

DIGITAL MATTE PAINTING

Matte painting is a technique by which a filmmaker substitutes some portion of a scene with an image created by an artist. For instance, if a scene requires a character to enter a huge castle, the director doesn't have to go to the expense of building a huge set. All the director needs to build is the door through which the actor passes, along with parts of the

THIS DIGITAL MATTE PAINTING *(above)* WAS COMBINED with a live-action scene *(below)* to create the illusion of a woman looking through a window toward a drowned, underwater village.

surrounding wall. An artist will then fill in the rest of the castle with a painting that exactly matches the set in texture, color, and lighting. Matte painting is an extraordinarily effective technique that has been used since the very earliest movies. It continued to be used nearly unchanged until recent times.

Traditional matte artists can create their paintings in several ways. They might create the painting, for instance, on a huge sheet of plate glass. They leave the live-action areas clear. The director would then shoot the live-action scene through the glass, filming the painting and the live-action scene at the same time. On the other hand, artists might do the matte

ARTIST SCOTT MCINNES DIGITALLY PAINTED THIS PIECE
of matte art for a motion picture.

painting on a large, rigid board, painting the live-action areas black. In this case, the director would film the painting and the live-action scene separately and combine it later.

In modern times, filmmakers use matte paintings by first scanning each frame of the segment of film that needs matte art. Then they transform the film into a series of digital images. Once the images are digital, they can be changed in any number of ways by a computer. Artists can create the matte painting separately in a computer program and then add it to the digital scene frame by frame. Or matte artists can paint directly onto the scene itself.

Digital artists create most matte paintings by using software such as Adobe Photoshop and Corel Painter™ X. They can also create digital matte paintings in three dimensions by using software such as Autodesk Maya or CINEMA 4D. Scenery and buildings will shift in perspective as the camera moves across a scene. This is impossible to achieve with traditional matte painting.

Working on individual frames allows matte artists to add or delete small details within the picture. For instance, the director might not have noticed an ugly sign. Rather than reshoot the scene, matte artists can simply paint it out of each frame in which it appears. In this same way, digital artists can easily remove wires suspending models or actors. Flying scenes, where an actor is suspended above the floor by wires attached to a harness, are much safer to shoot. Filmmakers used to use the thinnest possible wires so the camera would not see them. With computers, much heavier, safer wires can be used and then deleted digitally.

Artists can also use real textures and objects in digital matte paintings by simply copying from reference photos or from a frame of the film itself. If, for example, they need to copy a rock texture in a matte painting, artists need only to "cut and paste" the texture from a similar rock in the original frame. Artists don't have to carefully match textures and colors with paint as they did with traditional matte paintings.

The drawback to digital matte art is that it sometimes looks too realistic. Traditional matte painters tried to avoid this problem by only

DIGITAL ART

MATTE ARTIST PIETER SWUSTEN COMBINED SEVERAL
different elements *(top)* to complete this matte painting *(bottom)* for a motion picture.

suggesting details with little blobs of paint. This more closely imitates how the human eye sees things. Showing every detail sharp and perfect gives some digital matte paintings a fake appearance that makes them easy to spot. The good digital matte artist tries just as hard as the traditional artist to create a scene the way the eye would actually see it.

Digital artists took matte painting to a whole new level in the film *Sky Captain and the World of Tomorrow* (2004). They created everything in the film except the actors and the few props around them. They created all the sets and all the locations. This saves a tremendous amount of money. Filmmakers can avoid the expense of building elaborate sets or traveling to distant locations.

SKY CAPTAIN AND THE WORLD OF TOMORROW USED CGI

imagery more than any other live-action movie in history. Almost all the sets and locations were created digitally, and the actors were inserted into the scenes later.

DIGITAL MAKEUP

As with every other aspect of special effects, makeup has also undergone a digital revolution. By digitizing the frames containing the actor, digital artists can change the actors just as for any other digital effect. They can create effects that would be otherwise dangerous or even impossible with traditional effects.

Actor Gary Sinise, for instance, played a double amputee in *Forrest Gump* (1994). The filmmakers used special effects to digitally "remove" his legs below his knees. Arnold Vosloo, playing the title character in *The Mummy* (1999) and its sequel, was radically altered by digital effects. Artists digitally removed pieces of his body, and you could see the background through holes that passed entirely through his face. Digital artists can add animated features—such as the snakelike arms of the alien Serleena in *Men in Black II* (2002). The character of Mr. Tumnus in *The Chronicles of Narnia* (2005) was an actor from the waist up and digital animation of a goatlike body from the waist down.

Digital artists can also transform one character into another by morphing. Filmmakers used this effect throughout *X-Men* (2000), *X2* (2003), and *X-Men: The Last Stand* (2006) to create the shape-shifting Mystique. Morphing (from the word *metamorphosis*, a Greek word meaning "to change") involves selecting sets of corresponding points on each image. In morphing one face into another, these points might include eyes, lips, ears, and the outline of the head.

Based on these sets of points, the computer rearranges the selected pixels to transform the original image into the second via a series of intermediate images. The more similar the before and after images are, the smoother and more convincing the morph will be. Morphing between two human faces is easier than morphing between a human face and that of, say, an elephant. The first major motion picture to feature the effect was *Willow* (1988). Programs similar to those used for morphing can distort or warp an existing image. Computer artists can stretch or distort an actor's face or body like those of an animated cartoon character.

AN OBJECT (SUCH AS A HUMAN FACE) CAN BE

transformed, or morphed, into something entirely different. Points selected on the original image are matched to equivalent points on the new object and gradually altered until the transformation is complete.

EDITING

As important as its ability to create images is the computer's capability for combining images. In the past, this always involved combining images from two or more pieces of film onto one. However, each time you copy an image, its quality degrades, much like making a photocopy of a photocopy of a photocopy. (The difference in quality in different parts of a scene would often give away that a special effect was taking place.)

Each copy of a film is called a generation. Traditional special-effects artists aimed to use film removed from the original footage by as few generations as possible. The filmmakers tried to shoot all effects on a single strip of film, ideally using the original live-action footage. But the danger is that if something went wrong, the original would be ruined and they would have to reshoot everything. This could be very expensive and sometimes even impossible.

Digital images, on the other hand, can be copied hundreds of times. Each copy will not only be of the same quality as the original but absolutely identical to the original. Every element in a computer-generated scene looks as good as the original footage.

Modern digital special-effects techniques are found everywhere and not just in motion pictures. They are widely used in TV commercials, video games, and music videos as well. Hollywood-quality effects are not yet possible on the home or school computer. But amateur or student filmmakers can create small amounts of 3-D animation themselves.

LEVEL OF DETAIL

In both video games and movies, special-effects artists use a concept called level of detail (LOD) to avoid rendering what the eye will never perceive. In a video game, for instance, an oncoming car will probably begin its life as a simple cube. Then, as it approaches the viewer and becomes larger, a simple texture is applied, and it becomes a rough shape. Even closer, it requires complex geometry and detailed textures for a sense of realism. The same technique is used in motion pictures. Distant objects are not given any more detail than necessary. This imitates the way the human eye and brain see the world. You are simply not aware of detail in distant or background objects. Applying LOD saves a lot of time when rendering long sequences in a movie and creates a much more realistic scene.

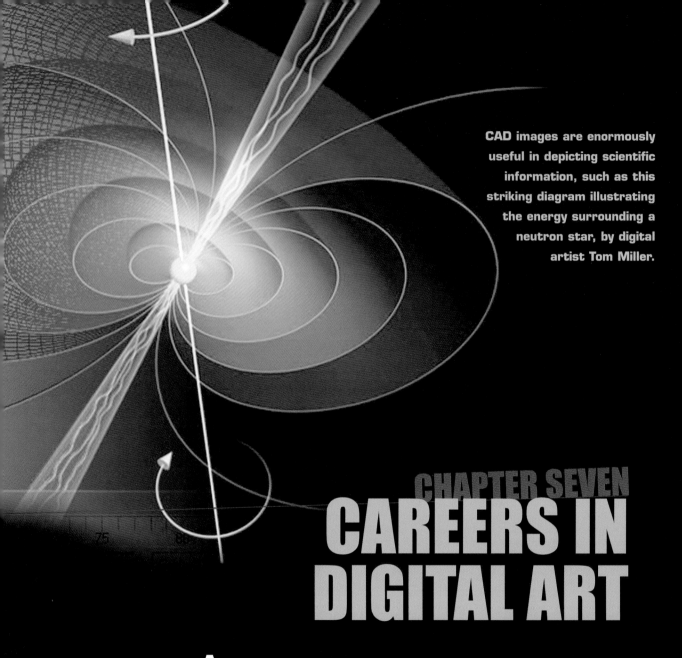

CAD images are enormously useful in depicting scientific information, such as this striking diagram illustrating the energy surrounding a neutron star, by digital artist Tom Miller.

CHAPTER SEVEN
CAREERS IN DIGITAL ART

As many potential careers in digital art exist as do different applications of digital art—from drafting to video games, from photo retouching to magazine illustration, and from motion picture special effects to comic books. The first qualification for being a digital artist is to be an artist. No software in the world is going to make up for a lack of ability or talent. You will need to study drawing, color, perspective, anatomy, light and shadow, and all the other things any traditional artist needs to know. The better you can draw and even paint, the better you will be at the mouse and keyboard. If you plan to go into any area of digital art, then be sure to include good courses in art in both high school and college.

GOING TO SCHOOL

A growing number of colleges, universities, and technical schools teach computer graphics and the many specialties used in film, television, and computer games. Some schools have much better programs than others. Look for one that has:

- A broad range of courses, including art, design, and other subjects as well as computing
- Faculty with actual work experience in the computer graphics (CG) industry
- Up-to-date computer equipment
- The respect of employers
- Evidence that graduates have been able to find good jobs

Most art colleges in the United States offer extensive programs in the digital arts, from illustration to animation to visual effects. Since these schools have made a specialty of art, they are often excellent choices for a thorough education in the field. Specialized art colleges, such as the Art Center College of Design (Pasadena, California) and the Columbus College of Art and Design (Columbus, Ohio) offer full-scale degree programs.

A number of new schools specialize exclusively in teaching digital art and visual effects. Some of these advertise heavily on television and elsewhere. Some of them are excellent and are run by seasoned, experienced professionals—such as the well-known DAVE (Digital Art and Visual Effects) School in Orlando, Florida—while others have much lower standards. Ask the same questions of these schools that you would any other.

A good way to enter the CG field is through an internship that provides both work experience and industry contacts while you are still in school. Major employers such as Industrial Light & Magic offer internships each year. These are much prized and very competitive. But lesser known companies also offer internships that may be easier to obtain.

GETTING A JOB

To apply for a job in CG, candidates present a demo reel showing examples of their best work. Students usually develop their demo reels during their school careers and internships.

The level of education most employers prefer to see is a bachelor of arts degree or, at the very least, a one- to two-year professional program for those who already have working experience. The skills required will vary greatly with each specialty. But most employers look for high-level computer skills and the ability to work in a competitive environment and as a team member.

Potential employers also look for a thorough knowledge of major software packages used in the industry, such as AliasStudio™, Autodesk Maya, 3ds Max, and LightWave 3D®, or of programming, networking, or administration. The aspiring digital painter must be familiar with software such as Adobe Illustrator, Adobe Photoshop, or Paint. Depending on your specialty, employers will look for knowledge of the principals of animation, attention to detail, artistic ability and judgment, creativity and imagination, and writing and storytelling. People with a combination of real artistic talent, strong computer skills, the ability to work with others and to communicate a vision, and an entrepreneurial knack have a distinct advantage.

While most computer graphics jobs are in large cities such as New York or Los Angeles, jobs in the digital arts can be found almost everywhere, depending on your specialty. Recently companies have been exporting a great deal of CG work—especially in animation—to other countries where wages are substantially lower. Industry experts predict that outsourcing will continue because the cost savings of using overseas workers are just too great to ignore. Therefore, the field will become more and more competitive.

The income you might expect to find as a newcomer in this field is usually fairly moderate, though, as is common in the entertainment industry. But the best and most sought-after people earn very high incomes indeed. Nationally, multimedia artists can earn up to ninety-four thousand dollars a year, though the average artist will earn less than this.

THIS DIGITAL PAINTING OF A FUTURISTIC CITY IS TYPICAL of the kind of work being done by professional commercial artists for motion pictures and advertising.

ANIMATION AND VISUAL EFFECTS CAREERS

What do animators and visual effects artists do? They create the visuals for games, movies, TV programs, advertisements, theme parks, and the Internet. Within these general areas are many fields of specialization: character animators, digital painters, lighting, render wranglers, and many more.

Ever since the earliest use of computer-generated imagery in films in the 1970s, CGI has become an overwhelming force in the motion picture industry. Almost every film produced contains at least one digitally manipulated image. Other films are entirely computer generated. In fact, some of the best, most memorable films are those using computer graphics to construct extremely vivid, larger-than-life virtual worlds. This requires the combined efforts of a large number of artists in different specialties. All these artists work together to convert the director's imagination into visual reality. As this field evolves and becomes more complex, jobs continue to become more specialized. Film producers no longer look for a "computer graphics person" but an

DIGITAL ART

"Autodesk Maya 3D texture artist."

Artists specializing in broadcast motion design create the graphics used in multimedia or television broadcasting to display sports statistics, animated logos, and advertising. Computer graphics programmers create

BECOMING A DIGITAL ARTIST

So you want to be a "digital artist"? As a long-time art-school teacher and professional illustrator, my advice to you is simple: First just be an artist.

I didn't have any choice. I was already in my twenties when the personal computer came of age. I was thirty-five when I bought my first one and learned to use it. I'd already had quite a few years of struggling to draw and paint with 'real' media, and I'm glad I did.

Drawing and painting on the computer is easier in some ways, but what ultimately makes you a "good" digital artist are the same things that have always made 'good' artists: the ability to draw, make a composition, use value and color, and most importantly be imaginative and have something to say.

In the end, I don't believe the medium is what matters. Think about it. You don't hear people saying, "That Van Gogh was sure a good *oil painter*,"

or "That Michelangelo sure could *cut marble*!" What will make your work special and unique, is what *you* bring to it, not the work of some software developer you happen to use.

Not that the work of those developers isn't amazing and creative in its own right. I'm in awe every day of the fantastic tools these talented folks have given us to create with. But in the end, it's up to us to create. Just knowing a program is no big deal.

Software is always changing, but size, shape, color, line, and form have been with us since the first artists we know of dragged earth against rock and made it so we could share their visions and worlds, even all these centuries later. Learn the time-proven basic skills visual artists need, and *practice, practice, practice.*

—Stewart McKissick, professor of illustration, Columbus (OH) College of Art and Design

the coding instructions that bring backgrounds and characters to life. Character animators analyze the way people and creatures move and use special software to create that movement on the screen.

Digital painters use traditional and digital painting techniques to create textures, flats, character patterns, and colors as well as to retouch and enhance computer renderings. Lighting specialists create the effects of light and shade that make animation look real. Render wranglers take the work of animators and artists and create the final images suitable for scanning onto film. Special-effects animators produce effects such as tornadoes, exploding asteroids, and collapsing buildings.

GAME DESIGN

Character and scenic designers for video and computer games are always in great demand. The skills, training, and work are almost exactly the same as those needed for digital animation and digital special effects in motion pictures. The computer or video game artist works closely with the game designer or developer—the person who actually writes the game itself.

The developers and the artists often work in teams. An art team may include artists who specialize only in designing characters, costumes, settings, and hardware. Good drawing skills are absolutely necessary, and although computer graphics skills are important, early development is often done with old-fashioned pencil and paper. Other artists specialize in recreating the designs in 3-D, creating textures and lighting, animating the characters, or creating special effects.

CAD

The CAD artist can work in a vast variety of fields and projects. CAD in architecture and engineering has all but replaced the traditional tools of the drafter. Architectural design and drafting can be both 2-D and 3-D—from the blueprints for a building to photo-realistic renderings of what the finished structure will look like. The architectural CAD artist may work on commercial buildings, residences, schools, structural engineering, and electrical design.

Civil engineering involves the planning, design, construction, and maintenance of structures as well as the altering of geography to suit human needs. Some of the areas in which a CAD artist may work include transportation (such as the design of highways), flood control, irrigation, water supplies, sewage disposal, land reclamation, buildings, bridges, dams, canals, and tunnels.

Aerospace engineering involves the design and manufacture of aircraft, rockets, and missiles. The aerospace CAD artist may be involved in the design of new airliners, military fighters and bombers, spacecraft, and satellites.

Mineral engineering—which includes mining, metallurgical (dealing with metals), and petroleum engineering—is concerned with removing minerals from the ground and converting them to pure forms. Other important branches of engineering are agricultural engineering, engineering physics, geological engineering, electronics, naval architecture and marine engineering, and nuclear engineering.

CAD IS USED BY

engineers and designers to illustrate new products and how they work. This drawing is by Stewart McKissick.

Electrical engineering is the fastest-growing specialty in recent years. It involves everything from designing power generators to computers.

ILLUSTRATION AND GRAPHIC ARTS

Most digital illustrators work freelance. They work for themselves or, occasionally, for small, independent studios. They do everything from photo retouching (one of the purposes for which Adobe Photoshop was originally created) to comic-book coloring and from magazine illustration to product design. Other digital artists work for large art studios that provide art for ad agencies and other clients.

We Grow in Ohio!

An educational
coloring book from the
Ohio Farm Bureau Federation

DIGITAL ARTIST STEWART MCKISSICK CREATED THE COLORFUL
advertising illustration *(above)*. Product designers have embraced digital art as a way to easily
and efficiently design and present new packaging for products, as in these examples by artist
Tom Miller *(below)*.

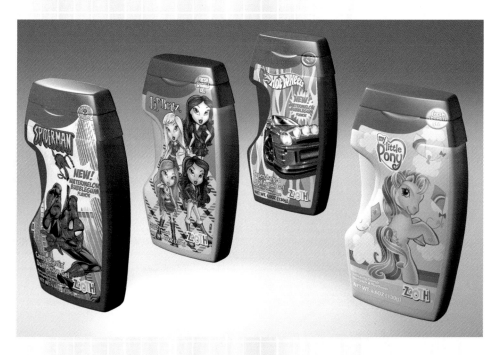

DIGITAL ART

DIGITAL ILLUSTRATORS—SUCH AS ERIC SPRAY, WHO

created this science-fiction illustration—are constantly finding new ways to express their ideas and new places to display them.

Each artist may specialize in a technique or subject matter. For instance, one may specialize in products such as automobiles or appliances, while another may specialize in fashion illustration or art depicting people. Very large ad agencies will often have their own in-house art departments. Greeting card publishers also hire a large number of artists.

THE FUTURE

As computer graphic technologies develop, artists will always find new, creative ways to use them. If history is any indication, artists will invent uses that the software and hardware designers never imagined. But that's the nature of the creative imagination: to see possibilities and new ways of doing things and to take something meant for one purpose and use it for something new and exciting. And the computer—probably the most versatile artist's tool ever created—is perfect for this kind of creativity.

GLOSSARY

bit: a unit of information; either a 0 or a 1

bitmap: a raster image composed of a rectangular grid of pixels

bump mapping: simulating three-dimensional textures on a three-dimensional model

byte: 8 bits

CAD (computer-aided drawing): using computer programs and systems to design detailed two- or three-dimensional models of physical objects, such as mechanical parts, buildings, and molecules

camera lucida: a drawing aid used by artists that projects an image of an object or scene onto drawing paper; similar to the camera obscura

camera obscura: a camera that uses a pinhole instead of a lens to project a scene onto a screen

cel: a sheet of transparent plastic on which an artist paints each frame of a traditional animated film

CGI: computer-generated imagery

cyberscanner: a device used to scan selected points on an object—such as a human being—and translate them into positional information for computer programs

digital art: using computers and computer software to create artwork

digitize: converting an image into digital form

encaustics: painting with hot wax

expressionism: a school of art that encourages artists to freely express their inner feelings and emotions

fractals: complex shapes and designs generated by mathematical formulas

giclee print: a method of creating very high-quality prints of digital art

graphics tablet: a device that allows digital artists to draw with a penlike stylus in much the same way they might be able to draw with a pencil or paint with a brush

hard drive: the main memory of a computer

harmonograph: a combination of two or more pendulums arranged in such a way that they create complex patterns on paper when they are swinging

image editors: any software program designed to manipulate or alter artwork or photos

layering: the process of separating different elements in a digital work of art so they can be worked on individually

lithography: a process of printing from ink applied to wet stone

morphing: the gradual change of one image into another

motion capture: recording the movements of a human or animal so a computer-generated figure can replicate them

naturalism: a school of art that insists on the realistic depiction of natural scenes and objects

oscilloscope: an electronic instrument that displays information as illuminated lines on a screen

particle systems: a technique that allows digital artists and animators to create the effect of fog, smoke, flame, etc.

pixels: the individual units of color on a computer screen

plotter: a machine that creates a drawing by moving a pen in two different axes

radiosity: a rendering method that simulates the way light reflects from one surface on to another

raster graphics: a method of rendering computer graphics that depends on pixels. While a raster image cannot be made larger without losing resolution, it is good for colors.

ray tracing: a rendering method that traces a ray of light from its source as it reflects and is refracted from different surfaces

real time: actual clock time. One minute in a computer game equals one minute of the player's time.

reflection: when light bounces off a surface

refraction: when light passes through a substance and its path is bent

refractive index: the degree to which light is refracted when passing through a substance

resolution: the amount of detail visible in an image. A low resolution image has little detail, while a high resolution image has a great deal of detail.

rotoscoping: tracing the movements of a human or animal

Spirograph: the trademark name of a toy manufactured by the Hasbro Corporation

surrealism: a school of art that intentionally uses distorted images and unlikely juxtapositions to create an impact on the viewer

symbolism: a school of art that uses images to represent abstract ideas and philosophies

texture: the apparent roughness or smoothness of an object

texture mapping: the technique of applying textures to a computer model

3-D model: computer art that simulates the qualities of a three-dimensional object

3-D rendering: creating an image that has the appearance of a three-dimensional object

vector graphics: a method of creating shapes in a computer that is independent of resolution. A vector image can be enlarged as much as needed without losing resolution.

wire frame: a method of rendering an object in the simplest possible way by outlining its shape with lines

SOURCE NOTES

6   Encyclopaedia Brittanica, 1972 ed., "Photographic Art," 938.

22   Linda Lauro-Lazin, "Computer Graphics in Context," n.d., http://pratt.edu/~llaurola/cg550/cg.htm (August 14, 2007).

60   Ed Bell, "Words From an Expert," sidebar written for *Digital Art: Painting with Pixels*.

65   Amelia LeBarron, "Designing This Book," sidebar written for *Digital Art: Painting with Pixels*.

102 Stewart McKissick, "Becoming a Digital Artist," sidebar written for *Digital Art: Painting with Pixels*.

SELECTED BIBLIOGRAPHY

Bentkowska-Kafel, Anna, Trish Cashen, and Hazel Gardiner. *Digital Art History*. London: Intellect Books, 2005.

Lovejoy, Margot. *Digital Currents: Art in the Electronic Age*. London: Routledge, 2004.

———. *Pos'odern Currents: Art and Artists in the Age of Electronic Media*. New York: Prentice-Hall, 1996.

Paul, Christiane. *Digital Art*. London: Thames & Hudson, 2003.

FOR FURTHER INFORMATION

BOOKS

Bidner, Jenni. *The Kids' Guide to Digital Photography: How to Shoot, Save, Play with & Print Your Digital Photos.* Asheville, NC: Lark Books, 2004.

Gardner, Garth. *Careers in Computer Graphics and Animation.* Washington, DC: GGC Publishing: 2001.

Grant, John, and Audre Vysniauskas. *Digital Art for the 21st Century.* London: AAPPL, 2004.

Hartas, Leo, and David Morns. *Game Art: The Graphic Art of Computer Games.* New York: Watson-Guptill, 2003.

Holtzman, Stephen. *Digital Mosaics, the Esthetics of Cyberspace.* New York: Simon & Schuster, 1997.

Hyland, Angus. *Pen and Mouse: Commercial Art and Digital Illustration.* New York: Watson-Guptill, 2001.

Karlow, Isaac Victor. *The Art of 3-D Computer Animation and Effects.* New York: Wiley, 2003.

Krensky, Stephen. *Comic Book Century: The History of American Comic Books.* Minneapolis: Twenty-First Century Books, 2008.

Miller, Ron. *Special Effects: An Introduction to Movie Magic.* Minneapolis: Twenty-First Century Books, 2006.

Spalter, Anne Morgan. *The Computer in the Visual Arts.* New York: Addison Wesley, 1998.

Withrow, Steven. *Toon Art: The Graphic Art of Digital Cartooning.* New York: Watson-Guptill, 2003.

WEBSITES

ACMSiggraph

http://www.siggraph.org

This is the official website for the world's largest annual exhibition of digital art and digital art resources.

The Amazing Harmonograph

http://www.airbrushmagic.com/harmonograph.htm

This website provides instructions for building and using your own harmonograph.

CG Explorer

http://www.cgexplorer.com/

This website provides links to many computer graphics, animation, and special-effects resources.

Cool Math

http://www.coolmath.com/fractals/gallery.htm

This is a good website about fractals with lots of examples as well as fractal generators that can be downloaded.

The Digital Artist

http://www.thedigitalartist.com

Resources and information for digital artists, including a detailed glossary of terms, are included on this website.

Digital Art Museum

http://dam.org/index.htm

This website includes a detailed timeline of the history of digital art as well as short biographies of leading digital artists.

Global Living: History of Digital Art

http://www.lastplace.com/LivingHistory/globalcart.htm

This website provides a comprehensive listing of digital history websites from around the world.

The History of CAD

http://imbinfo.imbdesign.net/CAD-History.htm

This website provides a comprehensive history of the development of CAD.

How Stuff Works

http://computer.howstuffworks.com/3dgraphics.htm

This Web page displays a detailed but simple explanation of how digital graphics work.

Planet Photoshop

http://www.planetphotoshop.com

This website includes easy tutorials for Adobe Photoshop users.

Plus Magazine

http://plus.maths.org/issue22/features/golden/

This is a detailed discussion about the golden ratio and its use in art.

Sand Pendulums

http://www.science.org.au/pi/book7/s7l1.pdf

This website provides instructions for making a simple sand pendulum, or harmonograph.

Spirograph

http://wordsmith.org/~anu/java/spirograph.html

A mathematician explains how the Spirograph works and provides a computer version that can be played with online or downloaded.

INDEX

PHOTO ACKNOWLEDGMENTS

The images in this book are used with permission of: © Dhabih Eng, p. 3; © Eric Spray, pp. 4, 54, 56, 101, 106; courtesy of Ron Miller, pp. 5, 14 (right), 17 (both), 25 (all), 86 (bottom), 91 (bottom); © Ron Miller, pp. 7, 9, 12, 14 (left), 15, 16, 18 (top), 26 (all), 27, 28 (all), 29 (all), 31, 34, 38, 39 (all), 40, 41 (all), 42, 43, 45, 49 (both), 50 (all), 52 (all), 53 (all), 62, 74, 75, 78, 86 (top), 88, 91 (top), 96; © Kenji Bliss, pp. 10, 51, 57; Library of Congress, pp. 18 (bottom), 19, 48; © Larry Cuba, p. 23; © Tom Miller, pp. 30, 36, 44, 64, 98, 105 (bottom); © Stewart McKissick, pp. 32, 58, 59, 63, 104, 105 (top); Ron Miller and *Scientific American*, p. 61; © Nate Piekos, pp. 66, 67 (both), 69; © Matt Johnson, p. 68 (both); © William Vaughn, pp. 70, 72 (all), 73, 77, 79, 80, 82, 83; courtesy of Universal Studios Licensing, LLLP (photo by Everett Collection), p. 89; © Scott McInnes, p. 92; © Pieter Swusten, p. 94; © Paramount Pictures. All rights reserved (photo by Photofest), p. 95 (both).
Front and back cover: © Dhabih Eng.

ABOUT THE AUTHOR

Ron Miller is the author and illustrator of many books, most of which have been about science, space, and astronomy. His award-winning books include *The Grand Tour* and *The History of Earth*. Among his nonfiction books for young people are *Special Effects*, *The Elements*, the Space Innovations series, and the World Beyond series, which received the 2003 American Institute of Physics Award in Physics and Astronomy. His book *The Art of Chesley Bonestell* won the 2002 Hugo Award for Best Non-Fiction. He has also designed space-themed postage stamps and has worked as an illustrator on several science-fiction movies, such as *Dune* and *Total Recall*.